**DEAR FELLOW MEMBER:**

Religion is popular today. Many "brands" of Christianity are being presented on radio and television and in printed form. As a result, even the most sincere believer is in danger of being confused or misled.

Therefore, I'm happy to be able to send you this study of the Epistle of 2 Peter. It defines what "the real thing" is as far as Christianity is concerned, tells how to avoid the dangers posed by heretics, and warns of the coming day of God's judgment.

So, please accept this book as my way of saying "THANK YOU" for your prayerful interest and support of Radio Bible Class this past year. We're encouraged to know you're standing with us as we proclaim the truth of God's Word through this Bible-teaching ministry.

Again, thank you, and may God richly bless you!

Richard W. De Haan
Teacher, RADIO BIBLE CLASS

# Studies in Second Peter

## by Richard W. De Haan

This book is designed for your personal reading pleasure and profit. It is also designed for group study. A leader's guide, entitled *How to Tell the Truth*, which is the Victor Book edition of *Studies in Second Peter*, is available from your local Christian bookstore or from the publisher at $1.25. (Catalog No. 6-2967)

**VICTOR BOOKS**

a division of SP Publications, Inc., Wheaton, Illinois
Offices also in Fullerton, California • Whitby, Ontario, Canada • London, England

A Victor Books mass market edition is entitled
**HOW TO TELL THE TRUTH**

Scripture quotations in this book are from *The New Scofield Reference Bible*, © 1967 by the Delegates of the Oxford University Press, Inc., New York. All quotations used by permission.

ISBN: 0-88207-750-3

VICTOR BOOKS
a division of SP Publications, Inc.
P. O. Box 1825 • Wheaton, Illinois 60187

# Contents

# *Preface*

The New Testament is marvelously alive and relevant—after almost 2,000 years! This exciting realization comes home to everyone who takes the *then* of the written Word and translates it into the *now* of the proclaimed Word. Peter wrote his second letter to encourage Christians, and to warn them of heretics and their false teachings. A similarity exists between the errors promoted during the first century and those which plague God's people today.

The devil knows he can do more harm to the cause of Christ through heresy within the Church than through persecution. History has shown that difficulties often drive Christians together, bring about greater dependence upon the Lord, and result in increasing effectiveness. This factor caused a Russian commissar, dismayed by the failure of his government to rid the country of the Christian faith, to make this observation: "Christianity is like a nail—the harder you strike it, the deeper it goes into the wood." Because of this, Satan often chooses false teachers rather than persecutors as his means of hindering the progress of the Church. And that's exactly why the message of 2 Peter should be familiar to every Christian. These biblical studies will help you to distinguish between truth and error, to be on guard against false teaching, and to stand firm for the faith.

A word of appreciation is due Clair Hess, David Egner, and Ronald Robinson for their editorial work, and to Lois Weber for typing the manuscript.

Richard W. De Haan
Herbert Vander Lugt

## 2 Peter 1:1-4

Simon Peter, a servant and an apostle of Jesus Christ, to them that have obtained like precious faith with us through the righteousness of God and our Savior, Jesus Christ:

Grace and peace be multiplied unto you through the knowledge of God, and of Jesus, our Lord,

According as His divine power hath given unto us all things that pertain unto life and godliness, through the knowledge of Him that hath called us to glory and virtue;

By which are given unto us exceedingly great and precious promises, that by these ye might be partakers of the divine nature, having escaped the corruption that is in the world through lust.

# 1

# A Supernatural Salvation

A well-known beverage company uses the simple yet effective slogan "It's the real thing" to inform the public that its product is the original—subtly suggesting that all others are inferior imitations. My purpose is not to discuss the relative merits of the various soft drinks on the market, and I'm not really sure it makes a great deal of difference which one you buy. I am profoundly convinced, however, that in the matter of salvation there is a great difference between the real thing and imitations or counterfeits. It's extremely important that you make the *right* choice. Your eternal destiny is at stake.

When the Apostle Peter wrote his second epistle, he was deeply concerned about the danger posed to true believers by imitators—men who presented themselves as Christians, but who in actuality were promoters of false religions which were fundamentally at variance with the teachings of the New Testament. The Church today faces the same threat. Prominent theologians are talking about "taking the myths out of the Bible." They don't believe in miracles, and they are not even sure that a personal God exists. False teachers from within the ranks of Christendom are confusing and hindering many believers. In addition, thousands of people who are sincerely trying to find salvation and grow spiritually are being led into false religious systems that do not present or produce a real, present, and personal salvation.

Peter wrote his second epistle to counteract the influence of false teaching. We therefore have the Spirit-inspired Word of God which tells us how to cope with the myriad of religions and pseudo-Christian groups prevalent in our contemporary world. Although the names and faces may change from generation to generation, the same erroneous teachings and skeptical attitudes appear again and again. These words from Peter, then, are not out of date. They have not lost their value. They can be trusted and applied today.

Our study begins with an analysis of 2 Peter 1:1-4. The Apostle laid the foundation of the entire epistle by establishing the fact that genuine salvation is a supernatural act—the work of God from start to finish. This alone distinguishes the real thing from its many counterfeits. The new birth involves a divine call, the implanting of a divine nature, and the impartation of divine power for successful Christian living.

## A Divine Call

The first supernatural element in salvation is that our call originates in God. Peter spoke of "the knowledge of Him that hath called us to glory and virtue" (2 Peter 1:3). We don't know for sure whether the word "Him" refers to the Father or the Son, for both are mentioned in verse 2. But it doesn't really matter. Since each is a coequal, eternal member of the Trinity, the meaning of the passage is clear: *God* has called us.

When Christians tell about their conversion, they often mention the overwhelming sense of God's call. They may tell of a Gospel tract that influenced them, or of a good friend whose changed life or spirit of kindness greatly impressed them. But they usually emphasize that it was God who singled them out and brought them to Himself.

The phrase "call of God" has two applications. First, it sometimes has reference to the general invitation of the Gospel, which is extended to everyone. Theologians often refer to this as the *general* call, pointing to passages like these: "Ho, every one that thirsteth, come to the waters, and he that hath no money; come, buy and eat; yea, come, buy wine and milk without money and without price" (Isa. 55:1). "And the Spirit and the bride say, Come. And let him that heareth say, Come. And let him that is athirst come. And whosoever will, let him take the water of life freely" (Rev. 22:17). The Bible contains many other loving appeals from God for sinners to accept the salvation He so freely offers.

When Peter spoke of our being "called to glory and virtue," however, he had in mind God's *specific* call. He referred to that act of God whereby a certain individual is led by the Holy Spirit to repentance and faith. We must remember that the initiative in salvation lies with God, not with us. The invitation to come to Christ could not be accepted by anyone if it weren't for the enlightening, convicting, and enabling work of the Holy Spirit. As a sinner, natural man is hostile toward God, spiritually blind, and dead in his sins. Paul declared, "There is *none* that understandeth, there is *none* that seeketh after God" (Rom. 3:11). He also said that "the natural man receiveth not the things of the Spirit of God; for they are foolishness unto him, neither can he know them, because they are spiritually discerned" (1 Cor. 2:14). He depicted unsaved people as "dead in trespasses and sins" (Eph. 2:1).

If left on his own, natural man would never seek God because man is spiritually blind and dead. He therefore needs more than the general invitation to receive Christ. The Holy Spirit must accompany the Gospel message with His supernatural work in opening sin-blinded eyes and giving the power to believe.

The biblical teaching of God's call is closely related to the doctrine of election and predestination. This connection is evident in the Book of Romans: "Moreover, whom He did *predestinate,* them He also called; and whom He *called,* them He also *justified;* and whom He justified, them He also *glorified*" (Rom. 8:30).

Yes, everyone whom God has predestined to be completely conformed to the image of His Son will respond to the Gospel. We don't need to discuss how God's foreknowledge is related to His predestination. This is one of the questions we'll never be able to solve completely as long as we are here on earth. But we do know this: When a person hears and believes the message of salvation, there is no doubt that this act of faith indicates that he has been called.

An old preacher revealed deep spiritual insight when he said, "I don't understand much about the doctrines of calling and election, but I'm sure of two things: I know that God loves everybody and invites them to Christ. And I also know that I was running away from Him as fast as I could, but He still found me and saved me."

Many Christians, looking back on their own experience, would say a hearty "Amen to that!" We're filled with gratitude as we reflect upon the mercy of God in calling us. We don't know *why* He did. It certainly wasn't because we were more deserving, or more intelligent, or came from a better family than those who haven't received Christ. For reasons we just don't understand, the Lord opened our eyes, overcame our wills, and enabled us to believe. An unknown hymnwriter expressed the wonder of this when he wrote:

> I sought the Lord, and afterward I knew
> He moved my soul to seek Him, seeking
>    me;
> It was not I that found, O Savior true;
> No, I was found of Thee.
>
> Thou didst reach forth Thy hand and mine
>    enfold;
> I walked and sank not on the stormy sea;
> 'Twas not so much that I of Thee took hold,
> As Thou, dear Lord, of me.
>
> I find, I walk, I love, but oh, the whole
> Of love is but my answer, Lord, to Thee!
> For Thou wert long beforehand with my
>    soul;
> Always Thou lovest me.

The truth of these words strengthens and encourages us, and fills our hearts with thankfulness. It assures us that what we have in Christ is indeed the real thing.

## A Divine Nature

The second supernatural element in our salvation is that we have been made "partakers of the divine nature" (2 Peter 1:4). The grammatical construction in the original languages indicates that when this occurred, we became "partakers of the divine nature" at the same time we "escaped the corruption that is in the world through lust." The moment a person receives Christ, he is delivered from this evil world system and becomes a partaker of the divine nature. It happens at the very beginning of the Christian experience, not at its completion.

The false teachers of Peter's day were saying that salvation is a gradual process of overcoming the corruption of this material world and becoming more like God. They taught that this transformation comes about through a long series of complicated religious rites and mystical experiences. They conceived of man's final state as a vague, impersonal, and nonmaterial immortality. Some of the present-day cults and Eastern religions are teaching a similar philosophy.

These heretics didn't understand that salvation is in three tenses. We *have been* saved from the *penalty* of sin—made members of God's family, given the new birth, declared righteous, and made citizens of heaven. We *are being* saved from sin's *power*—growing in grace and knowledge and becoming more Christlike. And we *shall be* perfectly holy someday, having been delivered from the very *presence* of sin. But this final goal is not something we achieve through our own effort. In all of its stages, salvation is a matter of grace. It is the work of God!

"But," I can hear someone asking, "what exactly was Peter referring to when he said that we are 'partakers of the divine nature'? Does that mean we are absorbed into God? Do we somehow become part of deity? Is it a physical thing, or is it mental? Does it come through meditation? What *does* it mean?"

A careful study of the Scriptures reveals that at least three factors are involved. First, all who believe in Christ are brought into union with Him. In John 15, the Lord spoke of Himself as the vine and His people as the branches, indicating that we are united with Him. The epistles often speak of us as being "in Christ." The Apostle Paul said that we who were dead in our sins have been made alive, and that we are already seated "in heavenly places in *Christ Jesus*" (Eph. 2:6). God so identifies us with Christ that everything He did and will do for us through His sinless life, His atoning death, and His glorious resurrection, is counted as ours. Death is no longer to be feared. The penalty for our sins has been paid, and the power of death has been broken, because we are one with the Lord Jesus in His death and resurrection. As a result, God can't condemn us, any more than He can condemn His sinless Son. It's as if we were already seated with Christ in heaven. What a wonderful thing to know!

Second, we are "partakers of the divine nature" through the new birth. The Bible teaches that the miracle of regeneration takes place the moment we put our trust in Christ. Jesus told Nicodemus, "Ye must be born again" (John 3:7). The Apostle Peter told Christians that they should love one another fervently, "Being born again, not of corruptible seed, but of incorruptible, by the Word of God, which liveth and abideth forever" (1 Peter 1:23). At our first birth we entered our parents' earthly family; in the second birth we were born from above by the Holy Spirit and entered God's family —a new community of born-again people.

Third, we are "partakers of the divine nature" through the presence of the indwelling Holy Spirit. This third person of the Trinity takes up residence in the body of a Christian the very moment he is born again. You don't need some kind of second blessing to receive His presence. Writing to the believers in Corinth, many of whom he had called "carnal," Paul said, "What? Know ye not that your body is the temple of the Holy Spirit who is in you, whom ye have of God, and ye are not your own?" (1 Cor. 6:19) The Holy Spirit indwells every believer from the moment he receives Christ.

The Apostle first emphasized the supernatural character of our salvation by saying that we are "partakers of the divine nature." There are at least three aspects of this spiritual reality. We have been made one with Christ, we have undergone a spiritual birth, and we have the Holy Spirit living in our bodies.

We may not always sense or feel the supernatural character of our salvation. We are still imperfect and subject to many failures. But the fact that we have been saved is just as real. Sometimes when we are feeling low, we must simply believe what God has promised in His Word. We need to remind ourselves of these grand and wonderful truths. This is done in conjunction with walking in obedience. When you submit to Christ in faith, the surety of God's supernatural power and presence will be yours. You will be able to say with the Apostle Paul, "I am crucified with Christ: nevertheless I live; yet not I, but Christ liveth in me; and the life which I now live in the flesh I live by the faith of the Son of God, who loved me and gave Himself for me" (Gal. 2:20).

## A Divine Power
The third supernatural element in our salvation is a sufficient supply of God's enabling power. Peter mentioned this when he said, "According as His divine power hath given unto us all things that pertain unto life and godliness, through the knowledge of Him that hath called us to glory and virtue" (2 Peter 1:3). All who have responded to God's supernatural call and have been made partakers of His nature are also given the power to live a joyful and victorious Christian life.

God doesn't abandon you the moment you're born again. Not at all! He has given you the power to be victorious over sin, and to be free from the hopelessness and fear that mark our world today. The salvation to which God has called you is complete: It begins when you receive Christ, continues in power throughout your Christian life, and culminates when you go to be with the Lord in the eternal Glory.

The fact that you have been guaranteed God's power, however, does not automatically mean that you will have a bulging purse, robust health, or a famous name. One can be in the best of physical condition, be world-renowned, and possess great riches, and still be miserable. But if you have the assurance of God's forgiveness, the consciousness of His eternal presence, the joy of answered prayer, the experience of His daily guidance, and the expectation of a glorious eternity in heaven, you can have the blessing of God's power in your life even in the midst of illness, great poverty, or anonymity. You'll be happy and confident as you abide in

Christ and yield to the leading of the Holy Spirit. So, read God's Word. Commune with Him in prayer. Take seriously the admonitions of the Bible and live in God's strength. As you do, your life will become more meaningful, and you'll be led into the beautiful assurance of faith.

Spiritual ineffectiveness is the inability to realize one's potential. In that sense, the Christian can be compared to an athlete who has tremendous physical ability but lacks the motivation to live up to his capabilities. A sportswriter recently listed the names of several baseball players who could be superstars, but who are actually just a little better than mediocre in their performance. Either because they have a bad attitude, or because they are unwilling to work on their weaknesses, they are a disappointment to those who expected greatness.

In the Christian realm, the Lord must also be grieved when He sees us fumbling and stumbling along. He has made it possible for us to play a winning game. He has brought us into union with Christ, given us a new nature, and sent the Holy Spirit to live in our bodies. He has made us members of a team destined to gain total victory over all the competition. Yet we live like losers. As we honestly evaluate ourselves, it's hard to see evidence that God's "divine power hath given unto us all things that pertain unto life and godliness" (2 Peter 1:3). Let's all avail ourselves of what the Lord has done *for* us so that His power can be seen flowing *through* us.

### The Real Thing
Biblical salvation bears the mark of God's supernatural activity from start to finish. Think of the miracles in its provision—the Virgin Birth of Jesus

Christ, His sinless life in the face of awesome temptation, His sacrificial death on the cross, and His bodily resurrection. Think of what happens when a person is saved! He responds to the work of the Holy Spirit, who removes sin's blindness and delivers him from the power of spiritual death. He becomes a "partaker of the divine nature" by being united with Christ, by undergoing a spiritual birth, and by receiving the Holy Spirit to live in his body. All of this makes him the possessor of a divine power which gives him everything he needs to live a triumphant Christian life. This is God's salvation! It is not some counterfeit, offering a vain hope. It's not a cheap copy, marketed by thoughtless men in an attempt to undersell the genuine product. It's the real thing!

Therefore, the person who has received Christ and now walks in fellowship with God can say with the Apostle Paul, "I know whom I have believed and am persuaded that He is able to keep that which I have committed unto Him against that day" (2 Tim. 1:12). Yes, you can know you are saved. God's redemption is genuine. It is indeed "the power of God unto salvation to everyone that believeth."

## 2 Peter 1:5-7

And beside this, giving all diligence, add to your faith virtue; and to virtue, knowledge;

And to knowledge, self-control; and to self-control, patience; and to patience, godliness;

And to godliness, brotherly kindness; and to brotherly kindness, love.

# 2

# A God-Honoring Life

It almost always happens! When you emphasize one side of a truth, somebody will either misunderstand or misapply what you say. Let a minister preach a sermon on the believer's security to comfort the fearful saints, and somewhere along the line you'll encounter the reaction, "This means I can curse and swear, rip and tear; but I'm just as sure of heaven as if I were already there."

Declare the truth that salvation is by grace through faith alone, and some people will think they should keep on sinning so they can take full advantage of God's grace. This is exactly how Paul's opponents responded when he proclaimed salvation by grace alone. He then had to correct their misconception (Rom. 6:1-11). One-sidedness and extremism are dominant human traits.

The Bible strikes a beautiful balance in the handling of seemingly paradoxical truths. It teaches God's sovereignty; but it also sets forth man's freedom and responsibility. It proclaims salvation by grace through faith alone; but it also instructs us to love God above all, and our neighbor as ourselves.

In the opening verses of 2 Peter 1, the Apostle

had clearly stated that salvation is the work of God from start to finish. He pointed out that the Lord calls us, that He implants the divine nature within us, and that He gives us His power in "all things that pertain unto life and godliness." But that is only one side of the coin. The next few verses of the chapter shift the focus of attention from the Lord to the individual believer, indicating that he is to live a godly life. The Lord has done His part in our salvation; our part is to follow Him in an obedient walk. Once we are born again, we are not to sit back in complacency and inactivity. We are "a new creation" (2 Cor. 5:17), and we view things differently than we did before. We want to serve God faithfully and glorify Him. We want to experience the wonderful blessings and benefits of being God's children.

Peter clearly spelled out what God expects of His followers. He told them to put forth every effort in demonstrating their faith as maturing believers. He then set forth the qualities of life God requires of His own. In this chapter, therefore, we will first look at the Lord's call to diligence. We will then consider the eight virtues of the Christian life we are to develop as we "grow in grace, and in the knowledge of our Lord and Savior, Jesus Christ" (2 Peter 3:18).

## Peter's Strong Command

When the Apostle told his readers that they should be "giving all diligence" to do their part in the Christian life, he used an expression that calls for an all-out effort. The two Greek words in this phrase are tremendously significant when used in combination. The first term indicates strenuous effort, like that of a runner who "gives it all he's got" as he approaches the finish line. The second comes from the noun *choregos,* which describes the wealthy patrons who financed elaborate religious plays in the ancient Greek world. These men often tried to outdo one another in generosity. They would provide extravagant equipment for the stage and pay out great sums of money to hire large choruses and good actors. It was a costly business for a man to sponsor a play, and because of this the word gradually came to mean someone who does an extremely costly deed. Peter therefore combined two words, one meaning great effort and another implying great cost, to stress that no labor is too hard and no price is too great in pursuing the God-honoring life.

At times we're overwhelmed by what God demands of us. We are easily discouraged as we try to live up to the Lord's expectations. We're almost overcome by a sense of frustration and failure.

But it's not necessary for any of us to give up. Ours is a *supernatural* salvation! It is God who is at work in the life of every believer. It is God who saved us. It is God who promised us victory over sin. It is God who called for spiritual maturity. It is God who will empower us to develop the virtues of a Christ-honoring life. And it is God who gives us untold blessings as we begin to put them into daily practice.

### The Qualities of a God-Honoring Life

The Christian is given a definite pattern to follow if he is to honor the Lord. Peter did not speak about godliness in vague generalities but with precision. The Bible never leaves us in the dark about God's will for our lives. It is specific and pointed as it expresses His demands. We will examine each of the eight qualities mentioned in verses 5-7, and consider the responsibilities of a born-again Christian. As we do, remember that God Himself has promised to help you develop them. *Faith*—The Christian life begins with belief in the Lord Jesus Christ as personal Savior. This faith is essential to salvation. Until a person has placed his trust in Jesus Christ, he can't even begin to please God.

Trusting Christ is what brings the forgiveness of sin, the removal of guilt, entrance into God's family, and life everlasting. Faith is the starting point. But it doesn't stop there. Faith is also the channel through which God's blessings flow into our lives day by day. Our trust in Christ is the dynamic of a successful walk with God. It's the hub around which every aspect of the Christian life revolves.

Many Christians do not consciously exercise faith in every situation they face. They have accepted Christ, confessing that He died for their sins, rose from the grave, ascended into heaven, and is coming again. They have the assurance that their sins are forgiven. They testify to having peace as they reflect on the day when they will die. But somehow they don't put that same trust into practice when they face the problems and frustrations of life. When they experience financial reversal, they panic instead of relying on their heavenly Father. When a loved one dies, they give in to almost uncontrollable grief and seem to forget that God loves them. In times of stress, they think only of themselves.

The believer in Christ should therefore reaffirm his unqualified trust in the Lord every day, whether he be basking in the sunlight of blessing or oppressed by trial and difficulty. When he does, he will experience the truth of these words: "Be anxious for nothing, but in everything, by prayer and supplication with thanksgiving, let your requests be made known unto God. And the peace of God, which passeth all understanding, shall keep your hearts and minds through Christ Jesus" (Phil. 4:6-7).

*Virtue*—The second mark of the God-honoring life is virtue. The Apostle said, "Add to your faith virtue" (2 Peter 1:5). In the New Testament, the Greek word translated "virtue" usually has reference to moral excellence, but its usage in the classical Greek adds a significant dimension. When an ancient Greek wanted to describe something that fulfilled its designed purpose, he ascribed this word to it. For instance, an especially surefooted, swift, and smooth-riding horse was called virtuous. Land labeled "virtuous" was usually fertile and productive. This descriptive term was applied to anything that perfectly fulfilled its designed purpose.

As believers we have a designed purpose—to be like Christ. We are to have as our goal a perfect conformity to "the image of His Son" beginning here and now. We can only make progress as we seek it in humble dependence upon the Lord. Then, as we overcome the flesh and develop the qualities of Christ Himself, we'll grow in virtue, for we'll be fulfilling the purpose for which we've been called.

*Knowledge*—The third characteristic of a God-honoring life is knowledge. We read, ". . . and to virtue, knowledge" (2 Peter 1:5). This does not refer to a profound conception of deep philosophical or theological matters, but to an understanding of basic Bible truths. A mastery of God's Word gives us solid grounding in the faith, enables us to make good choices, and arms us for victory over temptations and trials. God is the God of truth, and He has made Himself known in the Bible.

It follows, therefore, that every believer ought to be involved in personal Bible study. It's the best way to learn what the Scriptures have to say, and it is a source of strength and guidance in the daily walk with the Lord. One reason we have weak Christians in our churches is that so few spend time studying the Bible.

*Self-Control*—The fourth quality of the Christian life is self-control. Peter wrote: "and to knowledge, [add] self-control" (2 Peter 1:6). We are to control our desires and appetites rather than allow them to dominate us.

A lack of self-control is destructive both to the individual and to society. The growing number of alcoholics, the bulging prisons, the swelling number of aimless vagabonds, and the alarming increase in broken homes are undeniable evidences of man's failure in this vital area. The wisdom of the world has fallen far short in its efforts to teach men and women self-discipline.

The Gospel of Christ meets this desperate need. When a person believes in the Lord Jesus, he is given the power to exercise self-control. He has a new nature, and he possesses the indwelling Holy Spirit. Former drunkards and drug addicts have found that faith in Christ, reading God's Word, spending time in prayer, and submitting to the leading of the Holy Spirit have enabled them to conquer destructive habits. This mastery of self, bringing the body into subjection, should mark the life of every believer.

*Patience*—The Greek word translated "patience" can also be rendered "steadfastness." It carries the idea of having a positive, hopeful attitude even in the most bitter trials and sorrows. The patient believer is able to accept financial setback, sickness, disappointment, and even death as part of God's perfect plan for him. He can be steadfast, joyous, and victorious in every extreme situation, for his confidence rests securely in the Lord. He will count the adverse circumstances of life as blessings in disguise. And he will stave off deep feelings of despair, for his life is anchored in the deep conviction that God is all-powerful and good.

*Godliness*—The next term Peter used in his enumeration of the qualities of a maturing Christian is godliness. This term speaks primarily of reverence toward the Lord, but it also involves respect and concern for our fellowmen. A devout Christian will adopt the attitude of Christ and see his fellowmen as created in God's image. He'll be keenly aware of their feelings. And he'll do his best to honor the Lord in every relationship of life.

*Brotherly kindness*—It's not surprising that if a person is godly, he will develop a spirit of brotherly kindness. The word translated "brotherly kindness" is the Greek word *philadelphian,* which means literally "brother-love." The natural outflow of a godly heart is a willingness to bear one another's burdens and a helpful spirit in large and small matters. It implies that we should promote the welfare of our fellow-believers by refraining from gossip, prejudiced statements, divisiveness, and harsh criticism. A believer who practices brotherly kindness will be helpful and loyal. He will stand up for his fellow Christians like a boy who rushes to defend his younger brother.

*Love*—Even such a high virtue as brotherly kindness must have added to it yet another characteristic, that of love. The strongest word for love to be found in the New Testament is used in this passage. It is *agape* love, which springs from within the heart of a person without regard for the worthiness of its object. It's loving others like God loved us. He was moved with compassion and provided a way of redemption even though there was nothing admirable in us to draw His love. We were guilty and condemned sinners, "enemies of God" (Rom. 5:10), but the Lord loved us enough to send His Son to die for our sins.

As an expression of love and gratitude to Him, we are to manifest the same spirit toward others. We must seek their welfare, regardless of whether or not we see anything lovable in them. The phrase "love one another" occurs 12 times in the New Testament, clearly emphasizing the significance of this spiritual quality.

These, then, are the eight characteristics of a God-honoring life: faith, virtue, knowledge, self-control, patience, godliness, brotherly kindness, and love. What a list! If we possess and practice these eight qualities, our lives will reflect in every way the beauty of the Lord Jesus Christ. We will love God's Word and study it. We will have unfailing self-control and be victorious in times of trial. We will manifest a continual reverence toward God and respect our brothers and sisters in Christ. And we will be totally selfless, seeking to bring blessing and help to those around us.

### Get to Work!

The development of all of these virtues may seem to be an impossibility. Expressing faith, self-control, patience, and brotherly love all the time isn't easy. There are many pressures. We feel that people don't understand us. We're only human, after all.

Yet, God wants us to be growing. He expects us to be more spiritually mature now than we were a year ago—more loving, more knowledgeable of God's Word, more self-controlled. We have been instructed to give "all diligence" to developing a God-honoring life. It requires a strenuous effort— but it's worth it!

Perhaps you have experienced disappointment as you've attempted to live by faith. Don't give up. Remember, God is interested in every aspect of your life. He did not bring you to salvation to abandon you. He didn't leave you to try to develop godly virtues in your own human strength. He has sent the Holy Spirit to indwell you. He offers you the clear instruction of His Word. And He has promised you His power and grace to develop these characteristics in your life.

Therefore, *give all diligence*. Get to work! Strive to develop godly qualities and you'll be surprised at the way God honors your sincere dedication and earnest efforts.

## 2 Peter 1:8-11

For if these things be in you, and abound, they make you that ye shall neither be barren nor un fruitful in the knowledge of our Lord Jesus Christ.

But he that lacketh these things is blind and cannot see afar off, and hath forgotten that he was purged from his old sins.

Wherefore the rather, brethren, give diligence to make your calling and election sure; for if ye do these things, ye shall never fall.

For so an entrance shall be ministered unto you abundantly into the everlasting kingdom of our Lord and Savior, Jesus Christ.

# 3

# The Rewards of Godliness

It's always sad to see a man invest everything he has in a product or service and end up with nothing. Even the financial experts have no iron-clad guarantee that their investment programs will bring the returns they expected. And the most experienced businessmen cannot be 100 percent sure that a new venture will be successful.

In the Christian realm, however, we have the promise of God Himself that a life of faithful service to Him will produce a bountiful reward. The old hymn is true which says, "It Pays to Serve Jesus." The popular notion that the Christian life doesn't allow for fun or excitement is a gross misconception. Though a God-honoring life does not guarantee good health or a ripe old age, it does bring rich results, here and in the hereafter.

The Apostle Peter enumerated three benefits that accrue to the child of God who endeavors to achieve the qualities of holiness:

1. He will be given *a satisfying effectiveness* in living.

31

2. He will have *the wonderful confidence* that he is God's child.

3. He will receive *a glorious entrance* into the presence of Christ in heaven when his life on earth is finished.

The believer is given the *secure* promises of God. As Peter told us in his first epistle, a sure inheritance awaits us in glory, and we are being kept for it by the power of God. There are no crashes of the spiritual stock market; no absconded funds; no bad marketing campaigns. We can know with absolute certainty that God will reward our faithfulness. The benefits may not be important from a materialistic viewpoint, but to the child of God they are of inestimable value.

## A Gratifying Effectiveness

The first benefit of a God-honoring life is that it is satisfying and effective. The believer responds to his knowledge of Christ as Savior by developing qualities that give glory to the Lord and which result in a meaningful, victorious, and fruitful life. Speaking of the Christian walk, Peter said, "For if these things be in you, and abound, they make you that ye shall neither be barren nor unfruitful in the knowledge of our Lord Jesus Christ" (2 Peter 1:8). The obedient Christian is happy in serving the Lord. When the Apostle said that our lives will not be "barren," he used a word that can mean "idle" or "useless." When he went on to say that a person who lacks the eight moral characteristics (vv. 5-7) "cannot see afar off," he meant that that individual is living shortsightedly.

We are therefore reminded in these verses that the obedient Christian will be fruitful and effective, in contrast to the carnal believer who is spiritually myopic and whose life performs no useful purpose. So blind to eternal values are these individuals that they pay little attention, if any, to what awaits them.

Because of their disobedience, they are careless or indifferent about spiritual matters. They do not have a clear concept of the eternal truths of God's Word. Peter said that the Christian who lives like this has "forgotten that he was purged from his old sins" (v. 9). He has gone back to living the way he did before he was saved. He overlooks the fact that he has been delivered from sin's guilt and power by his faith in Jesus Christ. He has not realized the meaning of Paul's statement, "Sin hath no more dominion over you."

The believer who honors God in his conduct will avoid these undesirable consequences. His life will be fruitful, purposeful, and meaningful, making an impact for Christ wherever he goes. He will see spiritual truth clearly, and he will live triumphantly in the midst of life's trials and temptations.

## A Wonderful Confidence

The second reward of a believer who honors God is the absolute assurance that he is God's child, and that he will one day inherit the blessings of eternity. Peter referred to this when he said, "Wherefore the rather, brethren, give diligence to make your calling and election sure; for if ye do these things, ye shall never fall" (2 Peter 1:10). The Apostle had previously made reference to the believer's call (v. 3), teaching that all who trust Christ have been elected according to the Lord's foreknowledge. Yet in this verse we are told to make certain that we belong to the family of God.

What did Peter mean? How can we make our

calling and election sure? The answer is: by the way we live. Please don't misunderstand. What we do and how we live has nothing to do with *obtaining* salvation. We are saved by grace, completely apart from our own works. The Apostle Paul made this very clear when he told the Ephesians, "For by grace are ye saved through faith; and that not of yourselves, it is the gift of God—not of works, lest any man should boast" (Eph. 2:8-9). "Not of works" means there is nothing we can do to earn or merit our own salvation. We are saved solely by the grace of God through our faith in the Lord Jesus Christ who died for us. True believers are God's children because they have been born into the family of God through faith in His Son. John said, "But as many as received Him, to them gave He power to become the children of God, even to them that believe on His name" (John 1:12).

When a believer in Christ sincerely desires to please the Lord and does his best to obey His will, the Holy Spirit gives him that added inner assurance that he is a child of God. Writing to believers in Rome, the Apostle Paul said, "The Spirit Himself beareth witness with our spirit, that we are the children of God" (Rom. 8:16). So, as we live for Christ, we will know we are members of God's family because of the Spirit's witness deep inside. No Christian ever needs to go through life with the fear that he has not been accepted by God. Our calling is "made sure" by the fact that our behavior has changed.

Not only did Peter admonish his readers to certify their calling, but he added, "If ye do these things, ye shall never fall" (2 Peter 1:10). The expression "these things" very likely has reference to the eight qualities of the Christian life (vv. 5-7).

As we add to our faith virtue, knowledge, self-control, patience, godliness, brotherly kindness, and love, the reality of our new relationship with God is attested to in our hearts, and we are given the assurance that we shall "never fall."

The Greek word translated "fall" can mean "to stumble" or "to trip." Peter was not talking about Christians losing their salvation, but had in mind those moments of carelessness or extended periods of backsliding that sometimes plague the believer. Paul wrote in a similar vein to the believers at Corinth. He was determined to follow Christ diligently in all things, lest he would endanger the power or effectiveness of his labor for Christ. That's why he said, "But I keep under my body, and bring it into subjection, lest that by any means, when I have preached to others, I myself should be a castaway" (1 Cor. 9:27).

Graphic language is used here. The Apostle was determined to keep the appetites of his body under control, lest he be disapproved of God. He wasn't afraid of losing his standing in Christ but of forfeiting the blessings of service. He knew he couldn't lose his salvation, but he clearly recognized the possibility of being set aside and becoming useless as a servant of God if he should fall into sin. He was determined to discipline himself stringently so that he could continue serving Christ joyously and effectively.

Some Bible scholars interpret Peter's words, "If you do these things, you shall never fall," as an assurance that the God-honoring believer will not become apostate. They say that the Christian who follows the Lord in obedience will never be deceived into joining a Christ-denying religion or cult. They say that John taught the same truth: "But the anointing [the Holy Spirit] which ye have received of Him abideth in you, and ye need not that any man teach you; but as the same anointing teacheth you of all things, and is truth, and is no lie, and even as it hath taught you, ye shall abide in Him" (1 John 2:27).

A believer will be kept from falling into error because he has a built-in "heresy detector," the Holy Spirit—He will never deny Christ's deity, His atoning death, or His literal resurrection. There is no conflict between these passages. John's promise is not conditioned upon obedience, but Peter's is. It would seem best, therefore, to conclude that Peter and John were discussing different aspects of the same Christian doctrine. John was saying that through the indwelling Holy Spirit a true believer will be kept from apostasy. Peter was declaring that if a Christian walks in obedience to the Lord, he will never stumble, thereby losing his assurance, joy, and usefulness in God's service.

I wonder if Peter might have been thinking about that night, many years before, when he himself had stumbled. You will recall that on the eve of our Lord's crucifixion Peter had bravely declared that even if all others in the world would forsake the Lord Jesus, he would not. Just a short time later, however, at Pilate's judgment hall, Peter was heard vehemently denying three times that he knew the Lord. When Jesus looked at Peter, the faltering disciple went out and wept bitterly. If only he hadn't been so boastful! If only he hadn't lost his self-control. If only he hadn't been so afraid. If only. . . .

Peter stumbled because he chose to protect himself rather than be identified before the world as a disciple of Christ. Perhaps that sad experience was uppermost in his mind when he wrote the words: "If ye do these things, ye shall never fall." As you yield to and obey the Holy Spirit, He will keep you from falling.

## A Glorious Entrance

The third reward of a God-honoring life will be given the believer when he enters heaven. "For so an entrance shall be ministered unto you abundantly into the everlasting kingdom of our Lord and Savior, Jesus Christ" (2 Peter 1:11).

Every born-again believer will go to heaven. But Peter wrote that if a believer had diligently practiced the eight virtues of the Christian life, his entrance into heaven would be glorious indeed (v. 11). He'll hear commending words from the Savior whom he has loved and served.

The Bible teaches that every believer must someday stand before the Lord at the judgment seat of Christ. There his works will be examined, and the rewards will be given out. The Apostle Paul, writing to the Christians at Corinth, indicated this when he said, "For we must all appear before the judgment seat of Christ, that everyone may receive the things done in his body, according to that he hath done, whether it be good or bad" (2 Cor. 5:10).

Paul also told the Corinthians that "If any man's work abide which he hath built upon it, he shall receive a reward" (1 Cor. 3:14). Then he added, "If any man's work shall be burned, he shall suffer loss; but he himself shall be saved yet as by fire" (v. 15), referring to the judgment of the believer's works—not to his salvation, which could never be earned. Paul was speaking about that future time when Christ returns for His own, and the believer's life (the way he lives after being born again) is evaluated.

Rich spiritual rewards await the faithful Christian as he takes his place among the saints in heaven. But the disobedient believer's entrance into glory will be lacking in abundance. His reward will be smaller—or nothing at all. He will be "saved, yet as by fire."

The contrast between obedient and disobedient Christians as they enter heaven might be likened to the arrival of two ships into port after having encountered the same storm along the way. One is carelessly rigged, poorly manned, and badly commanded. Though it reaches the harbor, its cargo is gone, and its sails and masts have been blown away—a derelict hulk towed along by a steamer.

The other vessel arrives in port properly captained. All sails are set and flags proudly waving. Everything is in order and the cargo is secure.

Which vessel portrays your spiritual condition? If you have the graces mentioned by Peter (2 Peter 1:5-7), your entrance into Christ's presence will be rich and glorious. The Apostle said, "For so an entrance shall be ministered unto you abundantly into the everlasting kingdom of our Lord and Savior, Jesus Christ" (2 Peter 1:11). The choice is up to you.

### The Best is Yet to Be

You *can* live the kind of satisfying Christian life God expects of His children. It will be gratifying for you as you experience the growth and enjoy the blessings of the obedient walk of faith.

You will have the confidence of not being removed from within the realm of God's grace, no matter what may enter your life. Though you may stumble and fall, this does not mean that you've lost your salvation. Because you have placed your faith in the Lord Jesus Christ as your Savior, you are a member of God's family forever. God will not impatiently expel you from His kingdom because of temporary lapse or fall into sin. He is grieved when His children do not follow Him in obedience, but He has made ample provision for restoration to fellowship with Him. When you follow the injunction to confess your sin (1 John 1:9), He forgives you and restores you to fellowship.

The best is yet to be! Christians will meet again in heaven to enjoy forever the infinite perfection of God. What a prospect! As I reflect upon this glorious expectation, I am reminded of a story Charles Spurgeon, the famous 19th century preacher, often told. An aged man had just been examined by his physician, who said to the family, "I'm afraid he's seen his best days." They didn't think he heard, but he did. Opening his eyes and speaking in a remarkably strong voice, he replied, "Seen my best days? Doctor, you are wrong! My best days are still ahead. I am about to be given an abundant entrance into the everlasting kingdom of my Lord and Savior, Jesus Christ. Don't say I have seen my best days."

## 2 Peter 1:12-18

Wherefore, I will not be negligent to put you always in remembrance of these things, though ye know them, and are established in the present truth.

Yea, I think it fitting, as long as I am in this tabernacle, to stir you up by putting you in remembrance,

Knowing that shortly I must put off this my tabernacle, even as our Lord Jesus Christ hath shown me.

Moreover, I will endeavor that ye may be able, after my decease, to have these things always in remembrance.

For we have not followed cunningly devised fables when we made known unto you the power and coming of our Lord Jesus Christ, but were eyewitnesses of His majesty.

For He received from God, the Father, honor and glory, when there came such a voice to Him from the excellent glory, This is My beloved Son, in whom I am well pleased.

And this voice which came from heaven we heard, when we were with Him in the holy mount.

# 4

# Essential Elements of Faith

I talk with people who tell me they are Christians, but when I question them I find that they are vague in stating what they believe. They are half-hearted in their commitment and uncertain about the basis for their salvation. Their Christianity apparently means so little to them, and their lives are so unchanged that I sometimes wonder if they are really born again.

How different they are from the apostles and other leaders of the Christian faith down through the centuries! No one could doubt *their* salvation. They knew what they believed and their lives showed it. They stood for Christ with unwavering faith, sometimes in the face of severe persecution. The whole world was changed by their preaching and example. It was clear to everyone that their lives were founded on a bedrock of faith and truth, and that they were secure in their hope for the future.

God expects the same confidence and trust from His followers today. This is evident from 2 Peter

1:12-18, where the Apostle presented three basic qualities of the Christian life that should mark every believer: (1) a deep conviction of truth, (2) a confident hope for the future, (3) a firm basis for faith. These characteristics related to life become a challenge to strengthen and deepen faith, and to better equip us to face the test of an unbelieving world.

## A Deep Conviction of Truth

Peter first set forth the importance of the doctrine he and the other apostles had been teaching. Although he was reminding them of truths they already knew, he did so deliberately to arouse them to godly activity. "Wherefore, I will not be negligent to put you always in remembrance of these things, though ye know them, and are established in the present truth. Yea, I think it fitting, as long as I am in this tabernacle, *to stir you up* by putting you in remembrance" (2 Peter 1:12-13).

Peter obviously considered it important for every Christian to have a good understanding of Christian doctrine. His readers were acquainted with the truths of the Scriptures, but he was convinced that they needed continual reminders. He would not agree with our contemporaries who say, "It isn't important to teach doctrine. Just point people to Jesus Christ." But you can't lead someone to faith in the Lord Jesus without teaching some doctrine. The sinner must realize that Jesus is the Son of God, that He became a man so He could be our Savior, that He died to pay for our sins, and that He arose from the grave to break death's power.

Don't misunderstand. A person doesn't need a complete knowledge of all the doctrines about Christ and salvation before he can become a Christian. But some things are essential and the claim that doctrine is not important is sheer nonsense. If someone says, "I believe on Jesus," you have a right to ask him questions such as: "Who is Jesus?" "Why did He die on the Cross?" "Do you believe in the Resurrection?" If he responds by saying that Jesus was only an unfortunate carpenter of Nazareth who spoke many wonderful words of wisdom and was killed by people who didn't understand Him, you have good reason to start teaching him some doctrine. He just doesn't comprehend what the Bible says about Christ's person and work.

The need to understand the truths of the Bible does not stop when a person is saved. No believer will grow to experience the fullest measure of peace, joy, and victory unless his knowledge of the Bible increases steadily.

Actually, learning new truths is an exciting part of the Christian life. Finding out what the Bible says about Christ being both God and man, possessing both a divine and human nature, is a wonderful discovery to the believer. Learning about the intercessory ministry of Christ in heaven is a thrilling experience. What a comfort to know that He understands our tears and pain because He Himself suffered misunderstanding, endured the hurt of rejection, sorrowed at a graveside, and went through the physical agony of Calvary! How assuring to learn for the first time about the Holy Spirit! This third person of the blessed Trinity has given us new life, has made us members of the Body of Christ, and has taken up residence within us! How amazed the new Christian is when he understands the doctrine of justification, realizing that through faith he stands before God completely forgiven and fully accepted! How marvelous the realization that right now the Lord Jesus is preparing a home in heaven for all who know Him, and that at death we immediately will join Him in glory!

Some believers testify that when they first became Christians they were almost breathless with wonder and excitement as they discovered new truths by reading the Scriptures. It's like seeing the Grand Canyon for the first time. Its magnificence is so awesome that you just can't take it all in at once. As you stand there and gaze, you observe new beauties, each more exciting than the last. It seems that you will never comprehend it all!

Doctrine is of tremendous importance—first in reaching people with the Gospel, then in bringing spiritual growth. Peter taught that the basic truths of the Bible must be presented repeatedly—even to folks who already know them. This may seem strange to someone who is either unsaved or is just starting the Christian life. After all, a great mathematician doesn't need to review the multiplication tables. A person who has earned his doctorate in biology doesn't go back to his ninth-grade textbook.

The realm of the spiritual is different, however, because walking with God is more than an intellectual exercise. Since the will and emotions are also involved, we need continual nourishment and cleansing through the Word of God. If we don't study the Scriptures regularly, we will soon become carnal, worldly, and self-centered. The old, sinful nature will draw us away through the enticements of the world, the flesh, and the devil. A Christian who fails to read the Bible every day, seldom goes to church, finds discussion of doctrinal truth uninteresting, and just goes through the motions of praying is backsliding—whether he realizes it or not. Sooner or later he'll succumb to the temptations of sin, or find himself completely unprepared for a trying experience. Yes, every believer needs to hear the truths of the Christian faith over and over again. He will benefit from God's Word every time he reads it. How true the words of the hymn by A. Catherine Hankey:

> Tell me the story slowly
> That I may take it in,
> That wonderful redemption,
> God's remedy for sin.
> Tell me the story often,
> For I forget so soon;
> The early dew of morning
> Has passed away at noon.
>
> Tell me the same old story
> When you have cause to fear
> That this world's empty glory
> Is costing me too dear.
> Yes, and when that world's glory
> Is dawning on my soul,
> Tell me the old, old story:
> "Christ Jesus makes thee whole."

People sometimes remark that it's boring to re-read the same Bible passages, or to sit through sermons that review the same old Gospel truths. Others say they can't seem to remember what they have read or heard. If this describes you, very likely you are already in a backslidden state. The Christian who is in fellowship with the Lord experiences spiritual cleansing and a renewal of his love for Christ when he hears a sermon—even if the passage is familiar and he's "heard it all before." Similarly, when he reads a well-known Bible passage, he'll find depths of meaning or facets of truth he has never before discovered. He'll be strengthened and encouraged to walk closer with the Lord.

A young farmhand said he couldn't see much sense in continually reading the New Testament because he was already familiar with its general contents. He added, "I don't see why I have to remember the exact words as long as I know the main ideas."

The farmer for whom he worked did not answer him directly. Instead, he handed him a dirty bushel basket and said, "Let's go down to the creek and fill this with water." The young man dipped it in and pulled it out, only to have it drained in a matter of seconds. The man commanded, "Do it again." After the worker had repeated the act several times, the farmer said, "Look at the basket now. What has happened to it?" The lad replied, "It's clean." The wise man said, "That's what reading the Bible does. Even though you may not think you are learning anything new, and even if you can't repeat word for word what you read, you are being cleansed. That's why you need to read God's Word every day."

Don't rob yourself of the joy, the peace, the assurance, and the increasing conformity to Christ that can be yours through daily study of the Scriptures. Read the "old, old story" over and over again. Listen attentively as the pastor presents its truths week after week in the church. They'll give you comfort, strength, and victory.

## A Confident Hope

The second element of the life of faith presented in this passage is a wonderful and joyous assurance regarding the future. Peter wrote:

Yea, I think it fitting, as long as I am in this tabernacle, to stir you up by putting you in remembrance, knowing that shortly I must put off this my tabernacle, even as our Lord Jesus Christ hath shown me. Moreover, I will endeavor that ye may be able, after my decease, to have these things always in remembrance (2 Peter 1:13-15).

Peter was aware that he would soon be called upon to die a violent death. This didn't come as a surprise, for the Lord Jesus had told him about it some 30 years earlier. The Savior had warned him, "Verily, verily, I say unto thee, When thou wast young, thou girdest thyself, and walkedst where thou wouldest; but when thou shalt be old, thou shalt stretch forth thy hands, and another shall gird thee, and carry thee where thou wouldest not" (John 21:18).

Now, as Peter wrote his second epistle, he was convinced that the Lord's prediction would soon be fulfilled. He was more than 60 years old. Nero had begun a relentless persecution of believers. Arrest and execution awaited him; he was certain of that. He compared his body to a tent, a transitory dwelling place, and said he would soon be leaving it behind. He knew that when his earthly life was over, he would go to be with the Lord Jesus. His concern was not for himself, but for the Christian friends who would remain on earth. They would be persecuted by unbelievers and would be threatened by false teaching within their own circles. Therefore, he was filled with hope regarding his own destiny, and was completely unselfish in his love for the people he would leave behind. Peter was calm, confident, and selflessly occupied with the needs of others while awaiting his own arrest and execution which he said would follow.

Every Christian can be calm about the future, even about his own death. We don't need to fear the end of life, nor should we be afraid that the entire human race will become extinct through a worldwide disaster. Yet these are precisely the fears which have made our society so neurotic and obsessed with sex and violence. In actuality, most people are not outright atheists, and many believe in some kind of future existence. But our world system is naturalistic and materialistic. People are torn between a desire for life after death and a fear of judgment; between a feeling that how we live does matter, and a "what's the use" attitude because so many say that death ends all. Only the Christian can live above this mixture of wishes, hopes, and fears. Because he believes in Jesus Christ, he has a bright hope for the future. With the Apostle Peter, he will look upon death as a departure from the body—the temporary tent in which he now lives—to be with Christ in eternal glory.

## A Firm Basis For Faith

The third element of the life of faith is its solid foundation—a firsthand contact with the Lord Jesus. Peter made sure his readers did not think he was engaging in wishful thinking when he spoke so calmly of his approaching death. He emphatically declared that Christ's glory and return was not the product of his and the other apostles' imagination, but the truth based upon personal experience:

For we have not followed cunningly devised fables when we made known unto you the power and coming of our Lord Jesus Christ, but were eyewitnesses of His majesty. For He received from God, the Father, honor and glory, when there came such a voice to Him from the excellent glory, "This is My beloved Son, in whom I am well pleased." And this voice which came from heaven we heard, when we were with Him in the holy mount (2 Peter 1:16-18).

Peter referred to the Transfiguration because on the mountain he, with James and John, was given a glimpse of the coming glory of Jesus Christ at His return. The privileged three had walked up the slope of an unnamed mountain with the Savior, and when they reached the top, Christ began to pray. We are told that He was suddenly changed, for "the appearance of His countenance was altered, and His raiment was white and glistening" (Luke 9:29). The Gospel writers recorded by inspiration that His face and garments were shining with brilliance, sparkling with a whiteness beyond anything earthly. It was as if the resplendent glory of Christ as the eternal Son of God had enveloped Him. At that instant Moses and Elijah, great heroes of the past, appeared in glorified bodies and began talking with Jesus about His approaching death. Then a cloud came upon them all, and a voice was heard saying, "This is My beloved Son; hear Him." When the cloud lifted, Jesus was alone with His disciples.

You can be sure these three apostles never forgot that unique demonstration of Christ's deity! Peter's description of that experience is lifelike and filled with emotion! When he realized his days on earth were nearing an end, he thought of Christ's return. He relived that wonderful scene, teaching his brethren of their coming glory.

The Christian faith is not built on hearsay or legend. The story of Christ's life, death, resurrection, and ascension to heaven was not written by men who lived hundreds of years after the events. Archeological discoveries have proven what Christians have affirmed all along—that the New Testament was written by contemporaries of the Lord Jesus. The truths it sets forth were learned either directly from Christ or through the special ministry of the Holy Spirit. These divine precepts had all been put into writing before the first century ended. The apostles repeatedly affirmed the authenticity of what they wrote, referring to the fact that they had lived with Christ, had touched Him, and had carefully observed Him before and after His resurrection. Peter said, "For we have *not* followed cunningly devised fables when we made known unto you the power and coming of our Lord Jesus Christ, *but were eyewitnesses* of His majesty" (2 Peter 1:16).

Yes, God has given us a solid basis for our faith! The New Testament was written by contemporaries of the Lord Jesus. Even the enemies of the Gospel now acknowledge that this is true. Its accuracy is being vindicated by the best evaluation and scholarship, and its message still applies. Thousands of people testify that through Christ they have been delivered from bondage to lust, drugs, or alcohol. Hundreds of thousands witness to the inner peace and confidence in the future they have found through faith in Christ. The truth of the Gospel is confirmed historically, scientifically, and experientially. You can stake your life on it—and your eternal destiny!

### Believers Can Know

The person who truly believes in Jesus Christ as Savior and walks with Him in a life of faith will possess three basic characteristics. He'll be deeply convinced that what he believes is true. He'll be able to explain the basis of his faith, supported by Scripture passages. He will have the joyful assurance that death is but the beginning of the eternal glories of heaven in the presence of the Savior. And he'll know that his beliefs are based on events of history, recorded accurately in the Bible under the inspiration of the Holy Spirit.

Some reading these words may yet be unsure of what they believe, and fearful about the future. Their faith in the Lord Jesus Christ may not yet be grounded upon a vital, life-changing experience. They may not be sure that they are truly God's children and headed for heaven. If this is true, they need to make a serious decision regarding their life and receive the Lord Jesus Christ, beginning a systematic, daily study of God's Word. We all need to acquaint ourselves with the basic doctrines of the Christian faith. Then we will have the assurance of salvation and begin to grow spiritually as members of God's family.

## 2 Peter 1:19-21

We have also a more sure word of prophecy, unto which ye do well that ye take heed, as unto a light that shineth in a dark place, until the day dawn, and the day star arise in your hearts;

Knowing this first, that no prophecy of the Scripture is of any private interpretation.

For the prophecy came not at any time by the will of man, but holy men of God spoke as they were moved by the Holy Spirit.

# 5

# Grounded in
# the Old Testament

With all the new religious philosophies in the world today, and the many old traditions, how can we know for sure that Christians are right? Is there any concrete evidence for accepting the teachings of Christianity over another religious system? Can we be certain that if we do place our trust in Jesus Christ, our sins will be forgiven and we can be sure of an eternal home in heaven? How can we tell the truth from error?

The Apostle Peter gave us answers to these questions in the first chapter of his second epistle. First, he told of his own experience as one of the disciples who was with Christ on the mount of transfiguration. Then he indicated that the Old Testament Scriptures offer even better support for the claims of Jesus Christ to be the Son of God and Savior of the world.

The "more sure word of prophecy" Peter mentioned in verse 19 is the Old Testament. Peter urged his readers to pay close attention to what its writers had to say, for it is a body of truth which can be trusted. Written by holy men of God under the control of the Holy Spirit, it is a beacon of light in the darkness of sin and error. Its prophetic fulfillments give undeniable evidence that Christ is the Messiah.

The historic Christian faith derives much of its doctrinal content from the New Testament, but the foreshadowings of the Gospel are rooted firmly in the Old Testament. Written under the inspiration of the same Holy Spirit, it is historically accurate and contains many detailed prophecies of the New Testament message. In these verses, therefore, Peter declared that the Old Testament revelation is a reliable witness to the truth of the claims of the Lord Jesus Christ, and he enumerated three facts that attest to the Old Testament's dependability: (1) inspiration, (2) illumination, and (3) confirmation. An examination of these important qualities will strengthen your faith in the Bible, and show you that it is worthy of the trust of everyone seeking spiritual help.

## Inspiration

The men who wrote the Old Testament recorded the word of God—not their own ideas. They wrote by inspiration of the Holy Spirit, which guaranteed that it was true and accurate. Peter described the relationship between the human authors and the Spirit when he said they "spoke as they were moved by the Holy Spirit." The Greek term translated "moved" is sometimes used to portray a ship in full sail, moving briskly over the water. This describes figuratively what happened to the Old Testament writers—they hoisted their sails and the Spirit of God filled them and moved them along as they wrote the Scriptures. They were receptive to the "breath of God" and obedient to His direction. Although each author retained his own style and vocabulary, they all received God's Word and were kept from error as they recorded it.

In referring to the Old Testament writers, John Calvin said, "They were moved, not because they were out of their minds, but because they dared nothing by themselves but only in obedience to the guidance of the Spirit, who held sway over their lips as in His own temple." (Quoted by Michael Green, *Tyndale New Testament Commentaries*, Grand Rapids: Eerdmans, p. 92.)

Bible scholars have debated the precise meaning of verse 20. "Knowing this first, that no prophecy of the Scripture is of any private interpretation" (2 Peter 1:20). Some believe that Peter was discussing the *interpretation* of the Bible, while others are convinced he was speaking of its *origination*.

Almost all evangelical commentaries agree that the word *hidias,* translated "private," means "its own." This term occurs 115 times in the New Testament and is always so rendered. They also acknowledge that the Greek word *epiluseos,* which appears as "interpretation" in the King James Version, is a difficult term to define. In the Gospel according to Mark it is translated "expounded" (4:34). In the Book of Acts it is rendered "be determined" (19:39) and refers to a decision to be made in a court of law. Therefore, we feel that the translation, "no prophecy of Scripture is of *its own unfolding*" is to be preferred. But this still doesn't tell us whether the "unfolding" speaks of origination or interpretation.

Scholars who believe Peter was referring to the interpretation of the Scriptures point out that the context refers to false teachers who did indeed misinterpret the Bible (see 2 Peter 2:1; 3:16). Since the Holy Spirit is referred to as the real author of the Scriptures (v. 21), it follows that He is the only true Interpreter (v. 20). Others believe this verse teaches that the Spirit-filled church alone is qualified to interpret the Scriptures. Still others prefer the translation "interpretation" over "origination," and see the term "its own" as meaning that no Scripture is to be interpreted in isolation from the rest of the Bible.

I agree that it is perfectly permissible to translate the Greek word *epiluseos* "interpretation," but it appears to me that the context and grammar do not support this rendering. In the preceding paragraph, Peter was *not* discussing Bible interpretation, but the *origin* and *trustworthiness* of the message he and the other apostles had proclaimed. He said that before God spoke at the transfiguration of Christ, He had already revealed Himself through the writings of the prophets. It would be out of place for Peter to inject the idea of the interpretation of the prophecies before he had concluded his discussion of their origination. Besides, according to the rules of Greek grammar, the clause "no Scripture is of its own unfolding" belongs with what precedes it, not with what follows.

In the context of this statement, Peter did not mention interpretation. Instead, he referred to the prophecies of the Old Testament, which he declared had come into being by the work of the Holy Spirit, who directed and controlled men of God as they wrote. John Calvin said in his commentary on 2 Peter, "They [the prophets] did not blab their inventions of their own accord or according to their own judgments." They waited on the Lord for information and His enabling power to put His thoughts into verbal form. This is in contrast to the false prophets of their day, who made up what they would say. The prophet Ezekiel pointed out the difference between true and false prophets when he wrote, "Woe unto the foolish prophets, that follow their own spirit, and have seen nothing!" (Ezek. 13:3)

But regardless of whether you see 2 Peter 1:20 as referring to the *origination* or the *interpretation* of the Bible, you'll find in this passage a strong affirmation that the Old Testament is indeed God's inspired word to mankind. Whether you read a lofty passage from Isaiah, a tender psalm, or a tragic story of sin and debauchery from the Book of Judges, you can be confident that you have before you the very Word of God. It *can* be trusted.

## Illumination

The second characteristic of Old Testament prophecy is that it gives light in the darkness. It brings spiritual *illumination* to those who are groping in the blindness of sin. Peter expressed it this way: "We have also a more sure word of prophecy, unto which ye do well that ye take heed, as unto a light that shineth in a dark place, until the day dawn, and the day star arise in your hearts" (2 Peter 1:19). The word translated "dark" in this passage may mean "dry or dirty." According to the Greek scholar Vincent, the term may carry with it "a subtle association of darkness with squalor, dryness, and general neglect." Our modern words "murky" and "dingy" express the idea well. As Christians, living in the filthiness of our sin-darkened world, we must therefore look to the Scriptures for light and illumination.

But how can Old Testament prophecies, written

by men of another culture several thousands of years ago, be relevant today?

First of all, they had much to say about the end of the world and the return of Jesus Christ. They gave us many details about our Savior's First Coming to earth, and they gave us even more information about His Second Coming. They spoke in specific terms about terrible judgments, great battles, and a glorious millennial kingdom. The Old Testament sends forth knowledge and hope as a beam of light into the gloomy despair of our degraded world. Prophecies are important to us, because everyone is interested in what lies ahead.

Second, the Old Testament Scriptures shine through the darkness because they tell exactly how God views us and our contemporaries. When the prophets denounced mankind as sinful and depraved, they were referring to our day as well as to their own. We may be more knowledgeable, have a more sophisticated theology, and live in a more advanced society, but the condemnations and warnings of the prophets still point to our perversity and lay bare our iniquity.

Peter's writings tell us that we are to take heed to the prophets "until the day dawn and the day star arise in your hearts." The expression "until the day dawn" and the term "Day Star" are references to Jesus Christ. He is called the "Morning Star" in the Book of Revelation (2:28; 22:16), and He is named "the Dayspring from on high" (Luke 1:78).

The Apostle is not speaking specifically about the Return of Christ. He indicated that the Day Star arises "in your hearts," thus referring to what takes place inside a person. The Second Coming, however, will be an actual, external event—not something individual or internal. I believe that Peter said "in your hearts" because he had in mind the transformation of life that takes place when the prophetic Scriptures are read and believed.

## Confirmation

The Old Testament writers were inspired, and they did bring the light of God's truth to the sin-darkened world. Peter stated that the fulfillment of these prophecies is also the *confirmation* of the apostles' witness to the deity of Jesus Christ. The precise manner in which the biblical predictions were fulfilled is a resounding verification of the truthfulness of the apostolic witness. It also gives assurance to all who believe in Christ that their salvation is indeed based on the truth.

Peter had emphasized (vv. 16-18) that the report of the apostles was authentic. He pointed out that they were giving firsthand reports of things they had personally seen and heard while they were with the Lord Jesus. When he stated that the disciples were "eyewitnesses of His majesty," he was speaking of that which happened to James, John, and himself on the mount of transfiguration.

Then Peter made this striking statement: "We have also a *more sure word* of prophecy. . . ." It seems he was saying, "We actually saw the majesty of Jesus Christ with our own eyes. We were with Him on the mount of transfiguration, and saw Him seated with Moses and Elijah. But we have a testimony that is even more certain than our own personal witness—the Old Testament. It's even more reliable than what we ourselves experienced!"

The many intricate details of the prophecies fulfilled in the life, ministry, and death of the Lord Jesus comprise an astounding witness to the authenticity of the Old Testament Scriptures. Someone has counted more than 300 specific messianic prophecies fulfilled in Christ's life and death. Here are a few examples:

*Micah 5:2*—The Messiah would be born in Bethlehem of Judea; His birth is recorded at that very place (Matt. 2:1).

*Isaiah 7:14*—Our Lord's virgin birth: Matthew and Luke declare that Mary was a virgin when Jesus was conceived and born (Matt. 1:20-25; Luke 1:26-31).

*Daniel 9:25*—Gabriel said that the time of the Messiah would be 483 years after the decree of Artaxerxes to restore Jerusalem, and the Savior came right on schedule.

Seven details concerning the betrayal of Jesus by Judas Iscariot were predicted in Zechariah 11. "And I said unto them, If ye think good, give me my price; and if not, forbear. So they weighed for my price thirty pieces of silver. And the Lord said unto me, Cast it unto the potter—a lordly price that I was prized at of them. And I took the thirty pieces of silver, and cast them to the potter in the house of the Lord" (vv. 12-13). Note the specific information provided by Zechariah: (1) Christ would be betrayed (2) by a friend (3) for 30 pieces of silver; (4) the coins would be silver; (5) the money would be thrown down; (6) it would be rejected for use in the house of the Lord; and (7) it would be used to buy a potter's field. If you read Matthew 27:3-10, you will find that every one of these things actually did happen during those crucial final hours of Christ's life—exactly as predicted centuries earlier.

A number of prophecies concerning the crucifixion of the Lord Jesus were fulfilled to the very letter. Here are several of them:

1. Isaiah 53:7—"He was oppressed, and He was afflicted, yet He opened not His mouth." In Matthew 27:12-14 we are told that Jesus made no answer to the accusations of the chief priest and elders, and that He was silent before Pilate.

2. Isaiah 50:6—"I gave My back to the smiters, and My cheeks to them that plucked off the hair; I hid not My face from shame and spitting." In Matthew 26:67 we read, "Then they spat in His face, and buffeted Him; and others smote Him with the palms of their hands."

3. Isaiah 53:12—"He was numbered with the transgressors." Matthew 27:38 says there were "two thieves crucified with Him, one on the right hand, and another on the left."

4. Psalm 22:18—"They part My garments among them, and cast lots upon My vesture." John 19:23-24 records the precise fulfillment of both aspects of this prophecy.

5. Psalm 22—the entire psalm is a preview of what happened to Christ on the Cross.

What can the skeptic say in view of these facts? If he is honest, he must admit that it is preposterous to assume that any living person could so shape and mold his life that he would fulfill all these prophecies to the letter. A person could not choose the place of his birth. He could not inveigle others to betray him, crucify him, thrust a spear into him, or gamble over his clothing. Such happenings could not have been staged. These are facts—fulfilled prophecies giving witness to the truth of the Gospel of Jesus Christ.

No wonder Peter declared with confidence, "We have a *more sure word* of prophecy."

## 2 Peter 2:1-3

But there were false prophets also among the people, even as there shall be false teachers among you, who secretly shall bring in destructive heresies, even denying the Lord that bought them, and bring upon themselves swift destruction.

And many shall follow their pernicious ways, by reason of whom the way of truth shall be evil spoken of.

And through covetousness shall they, with feigned words, make merchandise of you; whose judgment now for a long time lingereth not, and their destruction slumbereth not.

# 6

# The Dangers of Heresy

Peter's tone changed drastically in this chapter. Up to this point he has been optimistic and positive. He set forth the qualities of a God-honoring life, and presented the solid supernatural basis upon which our salvation is founded. But in this section Peter delivered a stern, harshly worded warning against heretical teaching. He foretold the coming of false teachers who would infiltrate the Church, promote erroneous doctrines, and live wickedly. Many believers, unable to tell the truth, would be led to adopt false beliefs and practices.

From Peter's prophetic statements, we can conclude that these apostates make outward professions of faith without having been genuinely converted. They join with true believers in the local church, and once entrenched, they drift further from righteousness and truth. They influence others to adopt their heretical teachings and evil ways of life. Peter stated that they even go so far as to use their religion to profit financially at the expense of God's people.

The Apostle's concern is dramatically realistic for today! Heretics pose a grave danger to the Church and should never be taken lightly. Peter dealt with them severely, exposing them for exactly what they were—unbelievers who distorted or denied the truth of God. Many today call themselves Christians, but reject basic biblical doctrines and encourage evil practices.

Heretics come in as many varieties as Campbell's soups. They range from those who claim to have received special visions to those who flatly reject the major doctrines of the Christian faith. But whoever they are, and to whatever degree they deviate from the truth, one thing is certain—all who pervert the fundamental teachings of Scripture must be counted as heretics and therefore viewed as enemies of the Gospel.

The cultists, for example, with their quasi-Christian approach and religious-sounding phrases, are leading thousands astray. The influential clergymen of some of the established denominations use their positions of power and prominence to promote godless, anti-biblical beliefs. Many young people are enticed to accept a twisted doctrine that has been substituted for scriptural truth. Carnal "sons of darkness" are always enticing God's people to follow their immoral behavior.

Heresy takes subtle forms. Its proponents often masquerade as genuine believers. We dare not for one moment minimize the threat posed by false teachers, nor make exception for anyone, no matter how slight the error in his teaching or practice may appear to be. Note Peter's harsh, straightforward, and blunt language, setting the pattern for our attitude toward heretics. "But there were *false prophets* also among the people, even as there shall be *false teachers* among you, who *secretly* shall bring in *destructive heresies,* even *denying* the Lord that bought them, and bring upon themselves swift *destruction.* And many shall follow their *pernicious ways,* by reason of whom the way of truth shall be *evil spoken of.* And through *covetousness* shall they, with *feigned words,* make merchandise of you; whose *judgment* now for a long time lingereth not, and *their destruction slumbereth not* (2 Peter 2:1-3, italics ours).

He minced no words; he spared no feelings. As a severe threat to the theological purity and spiritual power of the Church, these heretics were to be identified and repudiated.

The Apostle described heresy as *destructive, defiling,* and *defamatory.* The first step in learning how to handle a heretic, therefore, is to recognize the dangers of his teaching in order to arm ourselves against all who would beguile us through fair speech and impressive manner.

### Heresy Is Destructive

In the first verse of the chapter the apostle used a form of the word "destruction" twice, indicating the danger heretics pose to the Church. He said, "There shall be false teachers among you, who secretly shall bring in *destructive* heresies," and then added that they will "bring upon themselves swift *destruction.*" Peter did not mean, by this strong term, total annihilation. If any of God's creatures were no longer capable of fulfilling the purpose for which they were made, the Bible spoke of them as having been "destroyed." A Greek historian would say that a cavalry horse had been "destroyed" if the enemy severed a tendon to cripple it. In a very real sense, we can say today that a government official who corrupts himself so that he is impeached has been "destroyed," for he no longer can fulfill successfully the office for which he was elected.

What a person believes can bring him eternal life—or it can destroy him. This is the reason heresy is so dangerous, both for the one who promotes it and for the one who may be misled. Causing an individual to accept error could send him to everlasting hell. It's not enough just to believe in God. You must put your trust in the Lord Jesus Christ, who said, "I am the way, the truth, and the life; no man cometh unto the Father, but by Me" (John 14:6).

Religious beliefs are not mere intellectual abstractions designed for theological discussion or mental stimulation. They are matters of great importance that lead to eternal consequence. The Lord Jesus identified Himself as the only worthy object of faith when He said, "He that believeth on Me hath everlasting life" (John 6:47). He also gave this warning: "For if ye believe not that I am He, ye shall die in your sins" (John 8:34). And it is written, "He that believeth on Him [Christ] is not condemned; but he that believeth not is condemned already, because he hath not believed in the name of the only begotten Son of God" (John 3:18).

In using the word "believe," we are not talking about an intellectual commitment to a church creed or doctrinal statement. Nor are we referring to the declaration, "I believe the Bible is true" or, "I believe there must be a God somewhere." James wrote, "The demons also believe, and tremble" (James 2:19).

It's not enough to believe that the Lord exists, or even that He is loving and kind. In fact, that can be dangerous, for a general belief about God or an intellectual assent to truth is often made a substitute for *the real thing*. As a result, the person who accepts this false premise fails to trust Christ personally for salvation. All who view the Lord Jesus as a great moral hero or inspiring example, but who deny His deity, face eternal condemnation.

The Bible is specific in its teaching about Jesus Christ. It declares that He is God incarnate, "the Word made flesh," that He actually lived in history as a man, that He was buried, and that He "rose again the third day according to the Scriptures" (1 Cor. 15:3-4). These basic facts about the Lord Jesus must be accepted, affirmed, and appropriated personally if one is to experience salvation. To deny these tenets is heresy, and both the proponents of the error and those they influence are in serious danger.

Some people say that it doesn't make any difference what you believe, just as long as you believe in something. But they are dead wrong! False doctrine, even though it contains an element of truth about Christ, leads to destruction.

## Heresy Is Defiling

The second danger of heresy is that it defiles those who are deluded by it. Peter wrote, "And many shall follow their pernicious ways, by reason of whom the way of truth shall be evil spoken of" (2 Peter 2:2). The Greek word *aselgeia,* translated "pernicious ways," is a strong term conveying the idea of extreme debauchery. It expresses the most reckless and debased kind of unbridled lust and licentious living.

While we aren't sure what the specific sins were, we do know that the false doctrines fostered by some in the Early Church resulted in gross, immoral behavior. One erroneous philosophy, for example, taught that God is concerned about the soul but not the body. Its proponents claimed that since the body perishes at death, no one will be held accountable for the sins of the flesh. Can you imagine the wicked behavior that such a view would breed? A person could gratify any lustful desire he wanted without fear of ever facing judgment. This would give license to live as one pleased —and some in the Early Church apparently did exactly that.

Heretical teaching does not necessarily lead to extreme wickedness, however. Some who reject or distort certain doctrines live on a relatively high moral plane. Nevertheless, when a person denies basic truths like the deity of Christ, the blood atonement, the judgment of sinners, or the inspiration of the Bible, he is guilty of heresy. He poses a special danger to the purity of the Church, for he is subtly undermining the doctrine of God's holiness —the foundation for all morality.

Whenever a person loses sight of the absolutes of God's Word as the expression of His holiness, he's on a moral toboggan slide. Though his decline may begin slowly, it ends in a headlong plunge away from God's Word and into disobedience and sin. The fear of the Lord and the desire to please Him no longer restrain him. His own code of ethics is substituted for the precepts of God's Word and, humanly speaking, there is no stopping the trend. The teachings of heretics defile the moral purity of the Church. They lower the standards and threaten spiritual ruin for those they mislead.

## Heresy Is Defamatory

Not only are the heretics' teachings destructive and defiling, they are also defamatory to the cause of Christ. Speaking of these apostates, Peter wrote, "And many shall follow their pernicious ways, by reason of whom the way of truth shall be evil spoken of" (2 Peter 2:2). The "pernicious ways," the evil behavior of these false teachers and their followers, will give people outside of the Church a reason to despise and defame the name of Christ.

The language used here to describe the contempt engendered among unbelievers is strong indeed! The Greek word translated "evil spoken of" is *blasphemeo.* We get our term "blasphemy" from it. This implies that the promoters of false teaching cause the Gospel to be maligned, to be brought into reproach before the world. When those who claim to be Christians provide convenient excuses for evil behavior by their teaching and example, they actually are giving occasion for Satan's cohorts to slander or blaspheme the cause of Christ.

Another reason a pseudo-Christianity which rejects biblical truths is defamatory is that it has nothing satisfactory to offer people who have deep spiritual needs. This watered down version of the Christian faith is really just another philosophy— just another voice in the clamor of a godless world. It cannot bring deliverance from sin and guilt. It cannot bring hope to a dejected, defeated life. It cannot bring peace to a troubled heart.

When people of the world look upon churchgoers who live on the same moral level as their contemporaries, but who exhibit no peace or joy, they naturally conclude that the Gospel is a farce. Thus heretics and their teachings give cause for "the way of truth to be evil spoken of."

## Application

The stern warnings of this passage cannot be taken lightly. False teaching is running rampant throughout Christendom. Everything from a blatant denial of the Word of God to a subtle, slight departure from the truth can be found within the Church and its related institutions. The damage being done is pervasive and far-reaching and leads to eternal consequences.

Heed the danger signals given by Peter. If allowed free course within the Church, heretics will promote a philosophy that is destructive, defiling, and defamatory. They will keep some from receiving the Gospel of salvation by faith in Jesus Christ. They will entice God's people to follow their wicked example of sinful, fleshly living. And they will cause the holy name of Christ to be blasphemed.

Beware of all false teachers—even if their error is slight. Reject them as dangerous, both to you and to your church. Repudiate their teachings as untrue, and see them as a grave threat to God's people. Renounce their evil way of life as self-exalting and godless. When you do, you and your church will be kept free from doctrinal and moral impurity.

What we believe is of utmost importance! The Nazis accepted Hitler's mad teachings and plunged the world into a war that claimed the lives of millions. Hundreds of thousands today have wholeheartedly adopted the doctrine of Marx and Lenin; as a result, large segments of the earth's population are under the domination of atheistic Communism. Sadly, countless numbers of people have been misled by the false teachings of the world's major religions, and many others by a distorted Christianity. They all face eternal death unless they turn in faith to the Lord Jesus.

## 2 Peter 2:4-9

For if God spared not the angels that sinned, but cast them down to hell, and delivered them into chains of darkness, to be reserved unto judgment;

And spared not the old world, but saved Noah, the eighth person, a preacher of righteousness, bringing in the flood upon the world of the ungodly;

And, turning the cities of Sodom and Gomorrah into ashes, condemned them with an overthrow, making them an example unto those that after should live ungodly;

And delivered just Lot, vexed with the filthy manner of life of the wicked

(For that righteous man dwelling among them, in seeing and hearing, vexed his righteous soul from day to day with their unlawful deeds),

The Lord knoweth how to deliver the godly out of temptations, and to reserve the unjust unto the day of judgment to be punished.

# 7

# God's Judgment
# of Heretics

The last person on earth I'd want to be on that final judgment day is a heretic! To know the truth and to reject it is bad enough; but to teach error deliberately and lead those who accept it into eternal perdition is an evil of almost unimaginable magnitude. The Apostle Paul was speaking specifically of false teachers like that when he concluded his graphic picture of the depths of human depravity in the Book of Romans with the words, "Who, knowing the judgment of God, that they who commit such things are worthy of death, not only do the same but have pleasure in them that do them" (Rom. 1:32).

We are told that John Donne, the 17th century preacher who in his later years proclaimed the Gospel with such power that a contemporary described him as speaking "like an angel out of the clouds," advocated certain heretical ideas when he first went into the ministry. To his dying day he sorrowed over the "seeds of doubt and licentiousness" he had sown as a young minister. He wondered how many people had been led down the path to their eternal doom. Yes, the dissemination of false doctrine does more eternal damage than any other sin. I tremble when I think of the fate of heretics.

Peter was deeply disturbed by the false teachers of his day, and spoke solemnly of the punishment that awaited them. We read that they "bring upon themselves swift destruction" (2 Peter 2:1), and their "judgment now for a long time lingereth not, and their destruction slumbereth not" (v. 3). This is a reminder that appearances may be deceiving. God is not idle, nor is He asleep. A few years of seeming impunity for the heretics must not be seen as a token that they will escape punishment from their sin.

Later in the passage the Apostle assured us that the Lord knows how to "reserve the unjust unto the day of judgment to be punished" (v. 9). The message of these verses is that all who introduce heresy into the Church will be judged by the Lord. God will not tolerate their deliberate distortions of the truth!

To illustrate the fate of false teachers, Peter turned to the annals of Old Testament history. He reminded his readers of three different groups who disobeyed the Lord and were severely judged because of it: (1) the angels who sinned, (2) the unbelievers destroyed in the flood, and (3) the citizens who perished in the destruction of Sodom and Gomorrah.

Since God dealt harshly with both heavenly and earthly creatures who disbelieved and disobeyed Him, we can be absolutely certain that He will punish every apostate. We're safe in concluding that all who insist upon following their "pernicious ways" will be judged by the Lord in fiery indignation.

## The Angels Who Sinned

The first illustration depicting God's judgment of heretics is the angels who were cast into hell. The Apostle wrote, "God spared not the angels that sinned, but cast them down to hell, and delivered them into chains of darkness, to be reserved unto judgment" (2 Peter 2:4). Peter did not tell us when this event took place, how many angels were involved, nor what act of wickedness called for such a drastic punishment. But we do know that at some point in history certain angels deliberately disobeyed God—and they didn't get away with it!

Bible scholars do not agree about the identity of these angels nor the time of their uprising. Some are convinced that Peter had in mind Satan's initial rebellion against God. This great insurrection is described in Isaiah 14 and Ezekiel 28. Isaiah's prophecy, though addressed to the earthly king of Babylon, used language that looks beyond the man in history to the leader of all the evil in the universe. He addressed him as "Lucifer," whom he called the "son of the morning" (14:12), and depicted him as seeking to dethrone God. Ezekiel's prophecy was against the king of Tyre, yet he spoke in such a way that he was obviously referring to this same angelic being. He called him the "anointed cherub that covereth" (28:14). Both prophets state that he was cast down from heaven. But we don't know if other angels sided with Satan in this revolt, for neither Isaiah nor Ezekiel indicate that other heavenly beings were involved.

We do know, however, that the devil now has a great army of wicked followers who assist him in his battle against God and His people. We are told by the Apostle Paul, "For we wrestle not against flesh and blood, but against principalities, against powers, against the rulers of the darkness of this world, against spiritual wickedness in high places" (Eph. 6:12). It's certainly not out of the realm of possibility, therefore, that a number of angels joined with Satan in his rebellion against the Lord. If so, Peter may have had them in mind, thinking of them as already cast out of heaven, already defeated by Christ, and already assigned to chains of darkness.

Other students of Scripture, however, believe that when Peter referred to the "angels that sinned," he had in mind "the sons of God" mentioned in Genesis 6. These beings are identified in Scripture only by this phrase. They "saw the daughters of men that they were fair; and they took them wives of all whom they chose" (Gen. 6:2). Scholars who maintain that these sons of God were the angels that sinned insist that the reason they cohabited with women was to produce a mongrel offspring of unusual power and wickedness. They say that this was a deliberate attempt, masterminded by Satan, to corrupt the human race and make the birth of the promised Messiah an impossibility.

God thwarted their attempt by destroying all living beings except Noah, who "found grace in the eyes of the Lord." Through his offspring the human race was able to continue uncorrupted.

To summarize this point, when Peter spoke of the "angels that sinned," he may have been referring to Satan's cohorts in his initial rebellion, or to a later effort by wicked angelic beings to pervert the human race and spoil redemption's plan.

Whichever you accept, the point is that these wicked beings were swiftly judged by the Lord. No one who rebels against the Almighty will escape His wrath forever. Just as surely as these creatures were judged by God, so all who promote heresy within Christendom will not escape His ultimate condemnation.

## The Unbelievers Destroyed in the Flood

The second illustration of God's judgment of heretics also took place in the days of Noah. Peter said that God "spared not the old world, but saved Noah, the eighth person, a preacher of righteousness, bringing in the flood upon the world of the ungodly" (2 Peter 2:5). The generations following Adam had become exceedingly sinful. Mankind had grown worse and worse, and we read in the Bible that the wickedness of man was so great that "every imagination of the thoughts of his heart was only evil continually" (Gen. 6:5). "The earth also was corrupt before God, and the earth was filled with violence" (6:11). People were living in gross immorality. Murder, cruelty, crime, lust, and injustice abounded. Except for Noah and his family, the entire race was dominated by sin and evil.

God therefore acted in judgment. He intervened in the affairs of men, "bringing in the flood upon the world of the ungodly" (2 Peter 2:5). Everyone was destroyed except Noah and his family.

As the Apostle continued, he added an element not included in the first illustration—that God judges with discrimination. He said that the Lord "spared not the old world, but saved Noah, the eighth person" (2 Peter 2:5). Noah, his wife, their three sons, and their wives were saved from a watery death. The Book of Genesis gives the reason: "Noah was a just man and perfect in his generations, and Noah walked with God" (Gen. 6:9). Because of his righteousness, "Noah found grace in the eyes of the Lord." As a result, he and his family were singled out from the rest of mankind to be spared. In the ark, the place of safety, they rode out the storm of God's wrath upon the wicked people of earth.

For 120 years, all the time the ship was being built, the people of that evil generation must have laughed and scoffed at Noah. He was called a preacher of righteousness; therefore, he must have pleaded with them to repent and warned them of the impending flood. But they didn't believe him. Then one day, God called Noah and his family into the ark. As promised, the sky darkened and the rains began to fall. Water gushed forth out of the earth. The angry flood rose higher and higher. The Lord Himself had shut the door of the ark. Righteous Noah and his family were safe inside, but all other human beings perished.

God's punishment of evildoers is certain, but His judgment is discriminating. Those who trust in Him are kept safe, while those who reject His will are destroyed.

### The Wicked of Sodom and Gomorrah
Peter gave a third example of divine judgment by reminding us of the devastation that fell upon the cities of Sodom and Gomorrah. He told us that the Lord turned them "into ashes, condemned them with an overthrow, making them an example unto those that after should live ungodly; and delivered just Lot, vexed with the filthy manner of life of the wicked" (2 Peter 2:6-7).

According to Ezekiel, the citizens of Sodom were

guilty of pride and immorality. The prophet recorded these words of God: "They were haughty, and committed abomination before Me" (Ezek. 16:50). Even today, the term "sodomite" has a connotation of gross evil and perversion. The inhabitants of Sodom and Gomorrah had become exceedingly depraved, especially in matters of sexual behavior. They had no concern at all for God's Word or His principles. As a result, God sent a holocaust of destruction. The cities were turned into ashes and now lie buried beneath the waters of the Dead Sea.

Again in this illustration, as in the preceding one, the Lord judged with discrimination. In punishing these two wicked cities, He distinguished between the righteous and the unrighteous. Peter reminded us of this comforting truth when he said that God "delivered just Lot, vexed with the filthy manner of life of the wicked" (2 Peter 2:7). His Spirit-inspired commentary informs us that even though Lot was in a backslidden condition while living in Sodom, he couldn't be comfortable there. A child of God, he could not be at peace in that wicked environment. That is the reason he was rescued before the fire and brimstone fell. He is an example of the truth of the words, "The Lord knoweth how to deliver the godly out of temptations, and to reserve the unjust unto the day of judgment to be punished" (2 Peter 2:9).

This principle of discrimination, however, does not always manifest itself exactly the same as at Sodom and Gomorrah. Believers who are faithful to Him may be killed in wars that come as an act of divine judgment. But God still rewards those who trust Him, and He punishes the wicked. We know that when a Christian dies, he will awaken in heaven, but the unbeliever enters the realm of the lost. Even though the distinction God makes between the righteous and the wicked may not be apparent in cataclysmic events, it is nevertheless a marvelous reality.

## God's Judgment Is Coming

In these days of increasing heresy, it is important to remember the three illustrations Peter used to show how the Lord will punish false teachers—the angels who sinned, the unbelievers destroyed in the flood, and the wicked of Sodom and Gomorrah. They serve as a stern warning that judgment awaits all who reject Christ. These actual historical events are a solemn reminder of God's wrath upon the disobedient. Their message is a billboard: "God's judgment is sure!"

Beware of those who scoff at the teaching of future judgment and ridicule the idea that God keeps an accurate account of the deeds of every individual. Don't follow them. If you do, you may share their doom. How foolish their attempts to deny the possibility of a day of judgment as described in the Bible! Man, puny little creature that he is, has now produced computers capable of keeping records on every human being upon the face of the earth. If he can do that, surely the great God who made and sustains all things can keep the books accurately! One day He will judge every person according to his works. Do not let people who have a small concept of God influence you to take the path of unbelief. If you listen to heretics you're in danger. If you join them in their wicked living and open defiance of the Almighty, you will stand with these wicked leaders when they face God's wrath!

But praise God, we do not have to conclude on a negative note. The Lord not only reserves the unjust to the day of judgment, He also delivers sinners from condemnation. The Bible tells us, "For God so loved the world, that He gave His only begotten Son, that whosoever believeth in Him should not perish, but have everlasting life. For God sent not His Son into the world to condemn the world, but that the world through Him might be saved. He that believeth on Him is not condemned; but he that believeth not is condemned already, because he hath not believed in the name of the only begotten Son of God" (John 3:16-18).

Salvation rather than condemnation awaits all who place their trust in Him.

# 2 Peter 2:10-18

But chiefly them that walk after the flesh in the lust of uncleanness, and despise government. Presumptuous are they; self-willed, they are not afraid to speak evil of dignities.

Whereas angels, who are greater in power and might, bring not railing accusation against them before the Lord.

But these, as natural brute beasts, made to be taken and destroyed, speak evil of the things that they understand not, and shall utterly perish in their own corruption,

And shall receive the reward of unrighteousness, as they that count it pleasure to revel in the daytime. Spots they are and blemishes, reveling with their own deceivings while they feast with you;

Having eyes full of adultery and that cannot cease from sin; beguiling unstable souls; an heart they have exercised with covetous practices; cursed children,

Who have forsaken the right way, and are gone astray, following the way of Balaam, the son of Beor, who loved the wages of unrighteousness,

But was rebuked for his iniquity; the dumb ass speaking with man's voice forbade the madness of the prophet.

These are wells without water, clouds that are carried with a tempest, to whom the mist of darkness is reserved forever.

For when they speak great swelling words of vanity, they allure through the lusts of the flesh, through much wantonness, those that are just escaping from them who live in error.

# 8

# The Consequences
# of Heresy

"Mind your own business!" said the man who was asked about the condition of his soul.

I suppose anyone, including myself, who has tried to talk to people about spiritual matters has received a similar answer or something like this: "What I believe is my own business!"

To some extent, the person who says that is right! After all, people are rational beings. They have a God-given will. They have the freedom to choose for themselves between the way of truth and the path of error. If they want to serve the devil, they can. If they wish to risk spending eternity in hell, they have the perfect right to do so, and you can't really stop them.

This doesn't mean, however, that as a Christian you should just stand by and watch someone walk the broad road that leads to everlasting destruction. You can pray for him. You can show him the love of Christ in what you say and do. And you can warn him of the terrible consequences of making the wrong choice.

The Lord God, speaking through the prophet Ezekiel, declared, "When I say unto the wicked, Thou shalt surely die; and thou givest him not warning, nor speakest to warn the wicked from his wicked way, to save his life, the same wicked man shall die in his iniquity; but his blood will I require at thine hand" (Ezek. 3:18). As believers in Christ, therefore, our solemn responsibility is to issue a warning when we see others threatened by impending danger, especially if it involves their spiritual welfare.

The Apostle Peter delivered just such a warning against the peril of heresy. He foresaw the day when the apostates would infiltrate the Church and lead many people astray. He spoke of the disillusionment that would follow for those who would be misled. Peter, deeply concerned about the threat such false teachers posed to the Church, described in detail their message, influence, motivation, and ultimate doom.

The Apostle spoke both harshly and specifically about the effect the erroneous teaching of heretics would have on God's people. He used some of the most scathing language of the entire New Testament to denounce them. He depicted them as living primarily for the gratification of their fleshly lusts. He said they would have no regard for law, and they would be totally lacking in respect for anything sacred. In fact, so contemptible would these heretics be that Peter described them as "natural brute beasts" (v. 12). Even today, all who choose to accept the apostates' proclamations are subjecting themselves to that which is dehumanizing, that which destroys everything worthwhile, and that which will ultimately mar all that is uplifting, beautiful, and pleasing to God.

Having begun this passage with a word of caution concerning heretics of the Church, Peter presents a vivid description of their way of life, speaking of it as insulting, revolting, and beguiling. A life-view which is contrary to the truth of God often results in the lowest forms of conduct.

## Insulting Behavior

The behavior of these apostates is first described as insulting to all who have a sense of morality and decency. They "walk after the flesh in the lust of uncleanness, and despise government. Presumptuous are they; self-willed, they are not afraid to speak evil of dignities. Whereas angels, who are greater in power and might, bring not railing accusation against them before the Lord" (2 Peter 2:10-11). The Apostle was not warning us about well-meaning but misguided people who sincerely want to find the truth and serve God. Rather, this reference is to men who have once known the truth but turned their backs on it. Having a proud, exalted opinion of themselves, they have no respect for those in power over them, whether they be religious or governmental. They claim the right to do as they please, making decisions in accordance with their own desires.

Peter went on to say that these godless leaders were "not afraid to speak evil of dignities." This means that they maligned the superiors to whom they were responsible. Had they accepted the fact that God takes note of everything man says, and that He will one day hold him accountable, they would have been more cautious.

In sharp contrast, we are reminded that angels, who are greater in power and might, are careful not to speak disparagingly of their superiors

(v. 11). In a parallel passage, Jude said that when Michael, the archangel, disputed with the devil over the body of Moses, he "dared not bring against him [Satan] a railing accusation, but said, The Lord rebuke thee" (Jude 9).

The difference between the holy angels of God and the false teachers Peter called "natural brute beasts" is that angels respect authority while the apostates do not. Today, as in the Early Church, many are guilty of insulting behavior. They show no regard for their fellowman or respect for those who hold positions of leadership because they have a philosophy of life which denies the biblical teaching about the one true and living God, and rejects any concept of a future accountability to Him.

Regrettably, religious leaders are often part of the problem. Many of them do not accept the scriptural presentation of God as a personal, righteous, and just Being. Proclaiming only His love, they consider any talk about His wrath as being hopelessly out of date. They portray the godly people of past generations who emphasized God's holiness and anger about sin as being slaves to a crippling fear. They scoff, for example, at the stern outlook of such groups as the Puritans, and all who believe in godly living.

But they are being historically inaccurate and unfair. Derogatory descriptions of the Puritans as unnecessarily fearful of God's wrath are dishonest. At times the Puritans were in fact severe, and they did make mistakes. In the later years of their movement some went to terrible extremes. But reading their great theologians or the printed copies of their sermons shows that along with the stress they gave to God's judgment is a bright and optimistic view of His love, His compassion, and His concern for

His people. They truly experienced the joy of the Lord. Though they are often pictured as wearing dark, somber clothing, in reality they wore bright, attractive colors. And their society generally was far more happy than ours. So don't let anyone tell you that reverence for God is an idea that belongs to the Dark Ages. In fact, if the wrath of God were preached more today, we'd all be better off. You may remember the saying, "He who fears God need fear nothing else." But we might add, "He who does not fear God needs to fear everything else."

Another familiar saying is equally true: "The man who bows down to nothing can never bear the burden of himself." People today, priding themselves because they have progressed beyond the fear of God, comprise the most nervous and neurotic generation that has ever lived. More and more people are seeking psychiatric help. A growing number are turning to alcohol as a crutch, hoping it will sustain them through the long hours of the day. Thousands keep on smoking cigarettes, in spite of the health warnings, because they need them to settle their nerves. And the suicide rate continues to rise, especially among younger adults.

A reverential awe of God would help change the picture. We ought to keep in mind the oft-quoted statement, "The fear of God quiets other fears." We should also remember that when a person loses the fear of God, he's taken a step on a downward course. The first effect of heretical teaching, therefore, is that it puts people on a pathway of behavior that insults the Lord's holiness.

## Revolting Behavior

Peter's scathing denunciation of the life-style of

those who reject God continued with these words: "And shall receive the reward of unrighteousness, as they that count it pleasure to revel in the daytime. Spots they are and blemishes, reveling with their own deceivings while they feast with you; having eyes full of adultery and that cannot cease from sin; beguiling unstable souls; an heart they have exercised with covetous practices" (2 Peter 2:13-14). The behavior of these people was absolutely revolting. The false teachers and their followers had lost all sense of shame. They practiced their evil ways in broad daylight!

Peter was offended by the barnyard morality of the heretics. Yet what he said is still true today. As in the days of the Early Church, there is much disgusting behavior which is the result of man's disregard of God. In our major cities, peddlers of pornographic literature have their shops open 24 hours a day. The X-rated movie houses run obscene films nonstop. Businesses openly exploit sex to sell their wares. Illicit affairs are commonplace. And abortions are on the increase.

While these practices are not usually considered as typical of the church crowd, it is true that some so-called liberated churchmen have contributed to the downward moral trend of society by their "situation ethics," their "new morality," and their permissive attitude toward sin. With the tacit approval of these religious leaders, many people have rushed headlong into a revolting pattern of behavior.

### Beguiling Behavior

Heretics within the Church often live in such a manner that they lead innocent, conscientious people astray. The Apostle described false teachers as "beguiling unstable souls" (2 Peter 2:14), and he further declared that they had filled their hearts with "covetous practices." He continued, "Who have forsaken the right way, and are gone astray, following the way of Balaam, the son of Beor, who loved the wages of unrighteousness, but was rebuked for his iniquity; the dumb ass speaking with man's voice forbade the madness of the prophet" (2 Peter 2:15-16).

The Bible doesn't record very much about the prophet Balaam, the man to whom Peter compared the heretics. He is mentioned in the Book of Numbers and several times in other Scripture passages. We learn that he possessed a prophetic gift which enabled him to predict the future and influence its accomplishment. He was at least somewhat acquainted with the Hebrew faith. He had been hired by Balak, king of Moab, to pronounce curses upon Israel and thus weaken its power. We are told how God prevented him from succeeding and caused him to do an about-face (Num. 22). Balaam then enunciated the blessing of the Lord upon the people of Israel, and it included a beautiful messianic prediction.

When he realized that he had failed to accomplish his original purpose, Balaam advised the Midianites to lure the Israelites into immorality and the worship of Baal. The men of Israel succumbed to this temptation, and some 24,000 of them died as a result of God's judgment. A short time later, Jewish soldiers killed Balaam along with the leaders of Midian. This wicked prophet wanted money so badly that he deliberately went against what he knew to be God's will. He was ready to see a nation destroyed for financial gain. And Peter said that the false teachers who were plaguing the

Church were really the same kind of people.

But that isn't all! Putting on airs, and speaking as educated authorities, false teachers deceive struggling believers who are just beginning to break away from the influence of evil men. Soon they are lured back into a sinful way of life. The counterfeit Christianity of these heretics serves the purposes of Satan, not the Lord of Glory.

Sad to say, many contemporary religious leaders fit the description Peter gave, and they deserve the Lord's condemnation. They use high-sounding phrases and make impressive claims, but they offer no true message of hope to lost sinners. Their words are empty air—leading unsuspecting souls down an immoral, godless road to hell! Like dried-up springs, they promise much, but in reality they give nothing at all!

Those who blindly follow such leaders and never accept the Savior are destined for eternal death, as victims of selfish, cruel impostors. These deceivers give hope of satisfaction, but in actuality they are "wells without water." They intentionally beguile people, leaving them to suffer the consequences of a God-rejecting life.

A minister with whom I am personally acquainted said that one day he called on a man who was almost helpless as a result of multiple sclerosis, and who had become deeply depressed because he had no assurance of his salvation. Though he had grown up in a Bible-preaching church and had accepted Christ as his Savior, he had become backslidden and married a woman who wasn't a Christian. They began attending a church where the Gospel was not preached, and soon they became members. A few years later he was stricken with his illness and the process of deterioration moved rapidly. The pastor openly acknowledged that he had no real message of hope for the dying man. Whenever he called, he could only tell a few humorous stories, hoping this would cheer him up. Besides this, the minister told the wife that she did not have to remain faithful to her invalid husband. She started dating other men, leaving her husband alone evening after evening.

This pastor almost destroyed the victim of multiple sclerosis by taking away all hope from him. When my minister friend called on this suffering man, he reminded him of the message he had heard in his childhood, and led him back to the place of peace and assurance. He then made arrangements for him to live in a Christian home where he received tender love and good care.

Any man who comes in the name of God but has nothing to offer a dying person should get out of the ministry. He ought to be honest enough to label himself an agnostic, for that's what he really is.

Don't be taken in by people who come as ministers of the Gospel, but who deny its power. Watch out for those who make great claims, but whose doctrine and life mark them as false teachers. Be on guard against men who do not fear the Lord or respect His Word, and who lead their victims astray for personal acclaim or financial gain.

## 2 Peter 2:19-22

While they promise them liberty, they themselves are the servants of corruption; for of whom a man is overcome, of the same is he brought in bondage.

For if, after they have escaped the pollutions of the world through the knowledge of the Lord and Savior, Jesus Christ, they are again entangled in it, and overcome, the latter end is worse with them than the beginning.

For it had been better for them not to have known the way of righteousness than, after they have known it, to turn from the holy commandment delivered unto them.

But it is happened unto them according to the true proverb, The dog is turned to his own vomit again; and the sow that was washed, to her wallowing in the mire.

# 9

# Recognize the Shackles of Heresy

Can you imagine what today's proponents of ecumenism would say to Peter about his epistle if they were to meet him? I can. I've heard their line of argument many times. They would express shock at his dogmatism, and decry his intolerant attitude as a remnant of the Dark Ages. They would insist that no one should sit in judgment of another man's religion, no matter how radical his ideas may seem. And they would conclude by saying, "After all, no one can be sure he is right in what he believes about God. So we might as well all try to get along."

I am sure that their protests would have no effect on Peter. That stalwart soldier of Christ would look these easygoing religionists right in the eye and declare that false teaching in the Church is not a matter to be taken lightly. He would point out that heresy can be devastating, especially to young Christians. He was well aware that people who are sincerely seeking answers to life's problems, but who are not well acquainted with the

Bible, are vulnerable to false doctrine. In addition, the Apostle would declare that we have a revelation from God by which we can discern truth from error. He would not apologize for having written in blunt, forthright terms about false teachers. And he would warn those who proposed a tolerance of error that if they did not repent and turn in faith to Christ, they would be in danger of the same condemnation as the wicked heretics.

Peter's exposé and warning of false teaching thus far in this epistle could be summarized by the following three principles he prescribed for handling the heretic: (1) recognize that he is dangerous, (2) acknowledge that he will be judged by the Lord, (3) repudiate and reject his sinful and self-centered way of life.

In the concluding verses of 2 Peter 2, the Apostle added a fourth guideline for handling heretics. He instructed us to keep in mind their true condition —in reality they are unhappy people destined to a sorry end. We certainly need to pray for wisdom to help them. But at the same time, we must be sure to keep them from corrupting our own beliefs. Immature believers should be warned about them. Social contacts which might be interpreted as indicating a measure of tacit approval should be carefully avoided. And we should commit ourselves anew to the Lord, asking the Holy Spirit to guard us from error and keep us untainted by the world.

Peter gives an honest appraisal of heretics (2 Peter 2:19-22). Although they promise liberty for their followers, they themselves are "servants of corruption." Evidently the false teachers the Apostle had in mind had once professed to be followers of Christ, but had returned to their lustful, wicked, selfish ways of life. They were dragging other believers down with them. Although they appeared to be Christians, they had not been born anew by the work of the Holy Spirit. They were still the slaves of sin.

If we are to confront the true state of false teachers within the Church, we must deal with several unavoidable questions: (1) Can one profess faith in Christ and still be lost? (2) What are the basic elements of salvation? (3) What ultimately happens to a heretic?

## Profession Without Possession

First of all, we must be fully aware that it is possible for a person to appear to be a Christian without having been born again. He may enter into a church and become involved in its activities; he may speak confidently of his faith in the Lord Jesus; he may serve willingly on various committees—but if his belief in Christ is a mere mental assent to certain biblical truths, he does not possess saving faith. The time will come when the external nature of his profession will begin to make itself known.

Since he is not genuinely converted, he will see no real reason to forsake the sins he enjoyed before getting involved in a church. The superficial character of his "changed" life will become increasingly evident. Finally he will return to his former life of sin, his heart hardened, his degraded state worse than before. Peter described this kind of person as follows: "For if, after they have escaped the pollutions of the world through the knowledge of the Lord and Savior, Jesus Christ, they are again entangled in it, and overcome, the latter end is worse with them than the beginning. For it had been better for them not to have known the way of righteousness than, after they have known it, to turn from the holy commandment delivered unto them" (2 Peter 2:20-21).

These verses raise an important question: Can a person who is born again ever lose his salvation? We believe in the eternal security of the believer, but what about Peter's statement that this apostate is worse off than ever? How can it be reconciled with these words of the Lord Jesus? "My sheep hear My voice, and I know them, and they follow Me. And I give unto them eternal life; and they shall never perish, neither shall any man pluck them out of My hand" (John 10:27-28). Is there a contradiction? Does Peter teach one thing and Christ another? Not at all! These passages are in complete harmony! *Profession of faith* in the Savior isn't necessarily *possession of salvation.* Not all who claim to be Christians are born-again followers of Christ. The person who denies the Lord Jesus after having made a profession of faith in Him, and turns again to his wicked way of life, very likely was never saved in the first place. Jesus informed His disciples of this possibility when He said: "Not every one that saith unto Me, 'Lord, Lord,' shall enter into the kingdom of heaven, but he that doeth the will of My Father, who is in heaven. Many will say to Me in that day, 'Lord, Lord, have we not prophesied in Thy name? And in Thy name have cast out demons? And in Thy name done many wonderful works?' And then I will profess unto them, I never knew you; depart from Me, ye that work iniquity" (Matt. 7:21-23).

By all appearances these men were born again. They had even worked miracles in Christ's name. But they had not received Him as their Savior from sin. To them Jesus will say, "I never knew you." He who is the discerner of hearts will know that they had not trusted in Him for salvation.

The potential for making a profession without having the possession is also seen in Jesus' parable of the sower recorded in Matthew 13. As the seed was sown, some of it fell on the hard surface of the pathway and was devoured by birds. Some fell on rocky ground where it sprouted, but the tender shoots soon died from lack of nourishment. Some of it fell on fertile soil and germinated, but the seedlings were choked out by weeds. Only one-fourth of the sower's work resulted in harvest.

In this parable, the seed symbolizes the Word of God, and the soil represents the hearts of men and women. The meaning is clear: Some people hear the Gospel message but never give it any consideration. Others go through the motions of accepting Christ and make a promising start but are not actually saved. They soon fall away because of some difficulty, or succumb to the allurements of the world. Certain people, however, do sincerely respond to the Word of God. They become fruitful Christians, bringing forth fruit, "some an hundredfold, some sixtyfold, some thirtyfold" (Matt. 13:8).

A seminary student, while visiting in a nursing home, met an aged, bedridden man who stopped him as soon as he began to talk. The elderly patient then presented his own summary of the Gospel. He did it with beautiful accuracy and clarity, and explained that he had once professed faith in Christ. But he went on to say that shortly after he started on the Christian walk, he decided to go his own way. After spending his life in sin, he knew that his death was near. But he had no desire to associate with members of God's family. When the seminarian asked him why, he admitted that perhaps he had not been sincere when he went through the motions of accepting Christ, even though his heart was tender at that time. He emphatically declared that now he had absolutely no inclination toward Christ. He said bitterly that if it would be his lot to go to hell, so be it. His attitude was one of stolid resignation to his fate, whatever it might be. His life illustrates that not everyone who goes forward in a meeting or in some other way responds to the Gospel has genuinely received Jesus Christ as his personal Savior.

Because of hidden mental reservations, pride, or some other reason, some people do not come to know Christ in a redemptive way. The proof of genuine conversion is found when a person who makes the profession goes on with the Lord throughout his life and produces spiritual fruit.

## The Basic Elements of Salvation

Having pointed out the possibility of making a profession of faith without being saved, we now confront a second question: "What are the basic elements in saving faith?" The faith that truly saves is characterized by two factors: first, the conviction that one is lost, under condemnation, unable to save himself; and second, a personal decision to accept Christ, with the belief that He died to pay the penalty for sin and arose to break its power.

*Acknowledge Your Lost Condition*—The first essential element of salvation is the frank admission that you are a condemned sinner and that you cannot save yourself. Jesus repeatedly emphasized this truth, but the religious leaders of His day wanted nothing to do with it. These self-appointed spiritual authorities looked upon themselves as being righteous because of their religiosity. Carefully observing intricate ritualistic forms and elaborate ceremonies, they prided themselves on a show of great piety and good works. They treated others with disdain, considering themselves to be spiritually superior. But our Lord declared, "I am not come to call the righteous, but sinners to repentance" (Matt. 9:13).

As long as a person thinks he is good enough to earn his own salvation, or feels that he can contribute something to merit its attainment, he isn't ready to place his trust in Christ. And if he doesn't come to the Lord Jesus as a helpless and condemned sinner, acknowledging his need for cleansing and forgiveness, he'll never be saved.

My father, Dr. M. R. De Haan, used to say: "You've got to get a man lost before you can get him saved." By that he meant that a person must come to the place that he realizes his inability to save himself before he will cast himself totally upon God's mercy as revealed in Christ.

*Make a Personal Decision*—The second essential element of saving faith is a personal decision to receive Christ. Consciously believing what the Bible says about Jesus' death on the Cross to pay the penalty for your sin, you must accept Him as your personal Savior. Just agreeing with a biblical doctrine expressed in church creeds is not enough. Even quoting Bible verses and saying they are true won't necessarily make you a Christian. You can be very orthodox, be faithful in church attendance, and live a good life—yes, you can even believe in God, but if you have never personally trusted the Lord Jesus Christ for your salvation, you are not a Christian.

No, my friend, it's not enough just to believe in God. It's not enough to give mental assent to the doctrines of Scripture. You must personally put your confidence in Christ, who said, "I am the way, the truth, and the life; no man cometh unto the Father, but by Me" (John 14:6).

I like the way someone summed it up by saying, "When you say Christ died, that's history. But when you say Christ died *for me,* that's salvation!"

So remember, mere profession is not possession. It's possible to make a commitment to Christianity just to please someone, to escape a difficult situation, or to give your life a spiritual dimension. It's even possible to be a faithful church member without ever being saved. If this is your case, then the words of John the Apostle could someday well apply: "They went out from us, but they were not of us; for if they had been of us, they would no doubt have continued with us; but they went out, that they might be made manifest that they were not all of us" (1 John 2:19). Outward profession is not necessarily inward possession. A genuine believer in the Lord Jesus, having acknowledged his sinfulness and received Christ, has the gift of eternal life. He will not become an apostate! He can *never* perish!

### Heresy Leads to Destruction

We are now ready to answer the third question, "What happens to heretics who persist in their distortion or rejection of the truth?" Peter said that they are "the servants of their own corruption" (v. 19). Then he added that their fate will be worse than those who never made any profession of faith in Christ at all. "For if, after they have escaped the pollutions of the world through the knowledge of the Lord and Savior, Jesus Christ, they are again entangled in it, and overcome, the latter end is worse with them than the beginning" (2 Peter 2:20).

What a solemn warning! A person may have heard the Word of God, outwardly professed belief in it, and even participated as a member of the fellowshiping community. But if he then deliberately disavows the truth and goes back to his old life pattern, he is going to be punished far more than the chief of a pagan tribe. Remember, great privilege always brings with it great responsibility!

Suppose a prominent man from a communist country defected and came to a free nation. Let's say that he kept on repeating how wonderful it is to live in this atmosphere of liberty. He seemed so sincere that he was given a responsible position which gave him access to classified information. But then he started to change his tune. He repudiated his professed love for his adopted land and returned to his former home. He had never had a real change of heart.

This illustration is only a faint reflection of what a person does to God when he professes faith in Christ, joins believers in fellowship, and then goes back to the old way. He has come face to face with the truth. He has seen what the Gospel can do in the lives of those who trust Jesus Christ. He has observed people being delivered from bondage to sin and fear through faith in the Lord Jesus. He has witnessed the power of God's salvation. And yet he will turn away from the Lord and go back to the vile way of life from which he has seen so many delivered. What an insult to God!

Peter described this kind of person with two graphic metaphors: a dog returning to its vomit and a pig returning to the mud. Though the language isn't very pleasant, we must heed the warning. It conveys a truth which must be heard. The Apostle wrote: "For it had been better for them not to have known the way of righteousness than, after they have known it, to turn from the holy commandment delivered unto them. But it is happened unto them according to the true proverb, The dog is turned to his own vomit again; and the sow that was washed, to her wallowing in the mire" (2 Peter 2:21-22).

A person cannot be confronted by the Word of God without making some kind of decision. Moral and spiritual neutrality is a virtual impossibility. Woe to the person who knows the way of righteousness, has walked in it, and then deliberately turns his back upon it!

Judas Iscariot was one who followed the teachings of Christ but did not accept them in his heart. He responded to the Savior's call and became one of the original Twelve Apostles. He was given the honor of keeping track of the money. Yet selfish greed ruled his heart. He listened to the Lord's teaching and observed His miracles, but apparently his primary concern was about the honor and riches he would obtain in the coming kingdom. Then, when it became apparent that Jesus was not going to set up the kingdom immediately, but was going by way of the Cross, Judas began pilfering from the meager treasury, and gradually turned against the Savior. He finally accepted blood money in a plot of betrayal against the best friend he ever had.

How tragic the result for the betrayer. The 30 pieces of silver he had coveted so intently did not give him satisfaction. A few hours after he had committed his vicious deed, wrenching feelings of guilt and shame swept over him. In bitter remorse he returned to the priests to give back his ill-gotten gain, but he was met only by their sneers and the laughter of hell. Overwhelmed with dark despair, he went out and committed suicide. In so doing, he plunged into even deeper darkness, for the Bible says he went "to his own place." Judas had heard the truth as it came from the lips of Jesus. He had responded to it outwardly, but he never really submitted to God's way of salvation. That refusal led to his destruction! Throughout history the name of Judas has stood as a warning to all who would exalt their own selfish desires and thoughts above the teaching of God's Word. He is a tragic yet persistent reminder that heresy is destructive!

If you don't know whether or not you are saved, the time for you to make sure is right now! It's dangerous to go on as a professing Christian without the certainty of salvation. You might become one of those Peter described as "servants of corruption" (v. 19), and be worse off than those who never heard the Gospel. You cannot remain neutral to the offer of the Savior. The call you are hearing today might never be heard again. The Bible says, "I have heard thee in a time accepted . . . behold, now is the accepted time; behold, now is the day of salvation" (2 Cor. 6:2).

## 2 Peter 3:1-7

This second epistle, beloved, I now write unto you, in both of which I stir up your pure minds by way of remembrance,

That ye may be mindful of the words which were spoken before by the holy prophets, and of the commandment of us, the apostles of the Lord and Savior;

Knowing this first, that there shall come in the last days scoffers, walking after their own lusts,

And saying, Where is the promise of His coming? For since the fathers fell asleep, all things continue as they were from the beginning of the creation.

For this they willingly are ignorant of, that by the word of God the heavens were of old, and the earth standing out of the water and in the water,

By which the world that then was, being overflowed with water, perished.

But the heavens and the earth which are now, by the same word are kept in store, reserved unto fire against the day of judgment and perdition of ungodly men.

# 10

# End-time Scoffers

We are members of a society that has become pre-occupied with the future. The world energy shortage, the threat of overpopulation, and the awesome potential of a nuclear holocaust have caused serious-thinking people to stop and take a close look at what lies ahead.

As a result, numerous books and articles on the subject of the future of man have flooded the market. Some represent the conscientious work of careful scholars who are genuinely seeking solutions to the problems that confront us. Some are highly speculative, the dramatic fantasies of irresponsible authors trying to make a fast buck at the expense of a frightened and gullible public. And others are the wild philosophies of a variety of pseudo-religious writers—mystics, astrologers, or self-appointed prophets seeking a following.

In general, the viewpoints of these futurists fall into two categories. Some are grossly unrealistic, painting glowing pictures of a glorious day when mankind will have solved all his problems and created a utopian world. Others are despairing and pessimistic, predicting a day when the earth will be a stark and silent planet, no sound echoing from the dusty ruins of a self-destroyed, lifeless globe.

To be honest, I'd probably accept one of these positions if I weren't a Christian. If I had to face the future without Christ, I'd either believe in some fantastic delusion, or I'd give up in total despair. But as a Bible believer, I can look ahead both optimistically and realistically. The Word of God has much to say about the last days, and we can often detect the difference between genuine Christians and counterfeits by the attitude they have toward these biblical declarations.

In the third chapter of his second epistle, Peter warned of the emergence of certain evil men. He referred to them as "scoffers" who would openly ridicule the promise of our Lord's return.

### The Question of the Scoffers

In taunting tones, the unbelievers of the last days will hurl this question at the followers of Christ: "Where is the promise of His coming? For since the fathers fell asleep, all things continue as they were from the beginning of the creation" (2 Peter 3:4).

We hear the same mocking question even today. The unbeliever, with a contemptuous smile and with the intent to discredit the faith of those who are "looking for that blessed hope, and the glorious appearing of the great God and our Savior, Jesus Christ," derides the Christian with statements like: What ever happened to Jesus' promise that He'd come again? He's been gone for more than 1900 years, and there's no sign He's ever going to return. Wouldn't you be better off to just forget about the whole thing?

Contempt for the promise of Christ's coming appears on high intellectual levels. Anything that smacks of the supernatural or miraculous is discredited without reasonable consideration. And secular university professors, with a sort of abstract amusement, merely "put up" with college students who express their belief in the Lord's return. Yet common folk doubt His coming as well. I recently heard of a self-appointed orator of meager education who got up in a city park to ridicule a nearby church. Its ministers had been preaching the imminent return of Christ for 50 years. "Jesus is just as dead as anyone else," the man cried. "He never arose from the grave. That preacher just wants your money. Forget about that Second Coming stuff. Do whatever you want. The only heaven or hell you'll ever get is what you make for yourselves here on earth."

We who believe in Christ and the Bible, however, should not be intimidated by mocking remarks or expressions of bemusement, because those who raise such questions are unknowingly fulfilling Peter's prophecy.

## The Ignorance of the Scoffers

These evil men are also revealing something about themselves. The Apostle indicated that they are actually showing their own ignorance. He said, "For this they willingly are ignorant of, that by the word of God the heavens were of old, and the earth standing out of the water and in the water, by which the world that then was, being overflowed with water, perished" (2 Peter 3:5-6). Men and women who ridicule the Second Coming of Christ are deliberately shutting their eyes to the truth of God's Word. They have closed their minds to important elements of Christianity, such as the account of the Creation recorded in Genesis. They also refuse to accept the reality of the flood of Noah's day.

So stubborn is the scoffing unbeliever that, in spite of the extreme inconsistencies of his own theory of naturalistic evolution, he refuses to consider seriously the biblical story of the Creation. He flippantly rules God out of the picture, unwilling to admit that the creationist could be right. He will not accept the possibility that "by the word of God" the heavens were created. He doesn't believe that one day at the beginning God separated the waters from the waters, and made the dry land to appear. In spite of overwhelming evidence from both geology and archeology, his mind is closed to the possibility that God made the heavens and the earth.

He also pooh-poohs the truthfulness of the Bible story of the flood. The idea that the earth was covered with water, and that God singled out one man to build a large craft and be safe within it, is to them mere legend. They don't want it to be true, because it would go against all their theories and presuppositions. So they scoff at it, shaking their heads in disbelief.

Yet the Bible teaches that we live in a universe that was created by a personal God. At key times in history, when mankind became extremely wicked, He sent His judgment upon it. The scoffers choose to ignore these important Bible truths because if they accept what the Bible says about Creation and believe its record of the great flood of Noah's day, they must accept the truth that Jesus Christ may come again. After all, if God did create this world by the word of His mouth, and did intervene in the affairs of men through the great cataclysmic event of the flood, who can deny

His interest in mankind today? And who can doubt that He will act again in judgment?

The wicked blasphemer therefore deliberately locks himself into a belief system which shuts out the personal and moral God of the Bible. Peter described this person as being willfully ignorant of the truth, and as destined to suffer the consequences of his stubborn disbelief.

## The Character of the Scoffers

Peter predicted that the rude behavior of these evil men would be in keeping with their character. He wrote, "Knowing this first, that there shall come in the last days scoffers, walking after their own lusts" (2 Peter 3:3). These words describe the Christ-rejecting mockers as wicked, selfish people, who will be interested only in gratifying their own fleshly desires.

Remember, the Apostle is not speaking here of the ordinary unbeliever. Many have never given God's claims serious consideration because they just aren't interested. They respect ministers and people who do believe, and generally are tolerant of the other person's viewpoint. On the contrary, Peter is referring to "scoffers"—people with a deep antagonism toward Christ and hatred of the Gospel. This kind of person is hostile to the truth, laughs at the beliefs of Christians, and makes fun of the Lord's return.

The reason for their attitude is not difficult to determine. These godless scoffers are "walking after their own lusts." They're offended by the moral demands of the Bible. They love their sinful way of life and have no intention of changing. So they give all kinds of excuses for rejecting the Word of God. They may present complicated systems of rationalization, but their underlying purpose is still the same: They don't want to give up their sin.

A statement by Aldous Huxley, widely read and famous atheist of this century, confirms this point. Late in his life he freely admitted that his dislike for the Scriptures and his derisive attacks upon the Christian faith stemmed from his desire to be free to sin. His objections were not philosophical or theological, for his underlying intent was to escape feelings of guilt. He wrote, "I had motives for not wanting the world to have a meaning; consequently assumed that it had not; and was able without any difficulty to find satisfying reasons for this assumption. The philosopher who finds no meaning for this world is not concerned exclusively with the problem of pure metaphysics; he is also concerned to prove there is no valid reason why he personally should not do as he wants to. . . . For myself, the philosophy of meaninglessness was essentially an instrument of liberation, sexual and political." (Aldous Huxley, *Ends and Means*, New York: Garland, pp. 270 ff.)

Huxley, who rejected Christianity because he wanted to live by his own standards and according to his own desires, is typical of those men and women of the last days who will ridicule the return of the Lord and walk "after their own lusts." This passage could be paraphrased to mean that these men's only guide in life was what they wanted for themselves. This was exactly what Aldous Huxley was admitting about himself.

This fact is important and should not be overlooked. As Christian parents, we should realize that it is not easy for a child to stand up for his faith when a teacher calls a Bible believer "stupid," "unscientific," or "a relic of the Dark Ages." It is our obligation to make sure our children understand that people who mock the Bible are doing so primarily because they don't want to live up to its demands. It's not a question of scholarship, but a matter of "walking after their own lusts." When young people from Christian homes realize this, they will remain firm when someone tries to undermine their faith in Christ. They will recognize that many people, rather than being open-minded, honest, and genuinely seeking the truth, have adopted a set of worldly standards and hold to a godless philosophy because these ideas best fit in with the way they want to live.

## The Doom of the Scoffers

Peter spoke plainly about what the future holds for them if they do not turn to Christ in faith. He wrote, "But the heavens and the earth which are now, by the same word are kept in store, reserved unto fire against the day of judgment and perdition of ungodly men" (2 Peter 3:7). The very same God who created the universe by the Word of His power, and who sent forth His judgment upon the wicked generation of Noah, is now holding everything together until the day when He shall destroy the universe by fire and punish the ungodly. Yes, for a time the scoffers are being allowed to ridicule God. They are laughing at the teaching that Jesus Christ is coming again. And it may even appear that they are getting away with their blasphemy. But their day of reckoning is sure to come! "The Lord is not slack concerning His promise, as some men count slackness, but is longsuffering toward us, not willing that any should perish, but that all should come to repentance. But the day of the Lord will come as a thief in the night, in which the heavens shall pass away with a great noise, and the elements shall melt with fervent heat; the earth also, and the works that are in it, shall be burned up" (2 Peter 3:9-10).

Notice the similarity between the flood of Noah's day and the judgment that awaits the mockers who laugh at the idea of Christ's return. Noah preached for 120 years while he was building the ark. Just imagine how that must have looked to his contemporaries. It took faith and courage for him to keep on working, and to continue warning men and women of the coming judgment. But obviously his audience paid no attention. Jesus said, "They were eating and drinking, marrying and giving in marriage, until the day that Noah entered into the ark, and knew not until the flood came, and took them all away" (Matt. 24:38-39). Not until the flood waters began pouring down from the sky and gushing up from the earth did these people realize that Noah's words were true. But then it was too late!

It's going to be the same in the last days. The coming of Christ will catch the wicked unawares. The taunting laughter of the scoffer will be turned into weeping. Righteousness will be vindicated; evil will be punished; God will be glorified. When the Lord Jesus returns in glory to judge the world and set up His kingdom, it will be His final supernatural act of intervention. He will frustrate the devil's last rebellion (Rev. 20:7-15). It is primarily to this event that Peter had reference when he wrote, "But the day of the Lord will come as a thief in the night, in which the heavens shall pass away with a great noise, and the elements shall melt with fervent heat; the earth also, and the works that are in it, shall be burned up" (2 Peter

3:10). This describes the end of the world system as we now know it.

## God Is on the Throne

Perhaps someone you know has scoffed at your belief in Christ's coming. Or maybe you wonder yourself why He has not yet returned. If so, a review of this chapter will help you. First, don't let the mocking words of scoffers trouble you! Those who make fun of the Scriptures and ridicule the teaching about Christ's return are unwittingly fulfilling Bible prophecy. We should not be surprised by their presence in the world, for God told us they would appear in the last days. Second, remember that scoffers are willfully ignorant of the promise of Christ's coming. They refuse to examine the evidence for the truthfulness of Bible history. They don't want to know the truth. Their motives are wrong and they have no desire to live righteously. They are only interested in finding a way to sin without fear of punishment.

Third, don't be discouraged by current events. God is on the throne. He's in charge of history. He will allow the forces of evil to go just so far, and then He will step in. In the end, righteousness will be honored and evil will be punished. This is our confidence, based upon what God has said in the Bible and what He has already done in the past. A wonderful day of vindication and glory is coming for all of His children.

## 2 Peter 3:8-10

But, beloved, be not ignorant of this one thing, that one day is with the Lord as a thousand years, and a thousand years as one day.

The Lord is not slack concerning His promise, as some men count slackness, but is longsuffering toward us, not willing that any should perish, but that all should come to repentance.

But the day of the Lord will come as a thief in the night, in which the heavens shall pass away with a great noise, and the elements shall melt with fervent heat; the earth also, and the works that are in it, shall be burned up.

# 11

# Answering Scoffers

"So Jesus Christ said He was coming again! Well, where is He? Almost 2000 years have gone by since He was here the first time. If He were really coming back, it seems He would have been here by now. Why don't you just forget about Him and face up to reality?"

Questions like these are often hurled at Christians by those who reject the biblical teaching of Christ's return. They discount His claims of being the Son of God, and sneer at the Gospel accounts of His resurrection from the grave. Furthermore, they don't believe He's in heaven now, and don't want to face realistically the possibility of His return to judge sin. Determined not to accept the promise of His coming and unwilling to submit to His moral demands, they mock those who believe that He will come again.

Adverse reactions to Christ's return should come as no surprise to God's people. Many centuries ago, the Apostle Peter predicted that the day would come when evil men would scoff at the promise of Christ's return (2 Peter 3:3-4). We should expect scoffers in these last days to make light of the promise of the Second Coming of Christ. It's the natural consequence of a rationalistic, materialistic, and skeptical age. And we cannot afford to take these mockers too lightly. Because their doubting questions seem logical, they pose a real threat to Christians not yet firmly grounded in the Word of God.

How can we answer these unbelievers? What can we say to the critics? Are we justified in continuing to look for the Savior's return even after so many years have passed?

Yes we are! The Bible, the inspired Word of God, is filled with promises that Jesus Christ will come again. In chapter 3 the Apostle spoke explicitly of skeptics and scoffers who would ridicule this precious truth, and he provided us with answers to their attempts to discredit it.

A detailed look at 2 Peter 3:8-10 can enlighten and strengthen your faith as you wait and watch for the Second Coming of Christ. Each of these three verses contains a pertinent observation relating to the doctrine of our Lord's return. They give us the correct perspective of the end-time as God sees it.

1. God's view of time is different from ours (v. 8).

2. God's love for man explains the seeming delay (v. 9).

3. God's prophetic declarations shall be realized (v. 10).

When Peter wrote this letter, he was well aware that the end of his life was near. He knew he would soon be executed for his faith in Christ. He also realized that after his death the people to whom he was writing would face persecution from outsiders, false teaching from within, and ridicule from unbelievers. He had given specific warnings about scoffers in the first seven verses of 2 Peter 3. As we noted previously, he discussed the taunting question of these mockers, described their self-centered character, their willful ignorance of the truth, and predicted the certainty of their doom. Then the Apostle added some thoughts which should encourage every believer today to "keep looking up" in spite of the sneering remarks of unbelievers.

## God's View of Time

The first truth Peter impressed upon his readers was that God looks at time far differently than we do. Those early Christians expected the Savior to return within a short time. When Peter wrote this letter, only 35 years had passed since Jesus had ascended into heaven. But much had happened in that brief period! Many believers had been ostracized by family and friends because of their faith. The winds of persecution from the Roman government were beginning to blow. The result was a real temptation to look at time from a human standpoint, rather than from the perspective of eternity. Peter therefore wrote, "But, beloved, be not ignorant of this one thing, that one day is with the Lord as a thousand years, and a thousand years as one day" (3:8). Mankind has a tendency to view 1,000 years or even 100 years as a long, long time. Sometimes even a month or two seems to stretch on endlessly. But this is not true of God. He who is without beginning and without end views a century or a millennium as really nothing at all. Remember, He has *always* existed. He is *not* limited by time.

This does not mean that He is unaware of the relationships of time. He surely knows the difference between one day and a thousand years! Rather, it indicates that He never needs to be in a hurry to get things done, and He is never fretful or impatient. He sees what will happen a thousand years from now just as clearly as we see what is occurring in our lives today. And He has everything under control.

Peter isn't giving us an equation by which God reckons time; it would be just as true to say that a million years is as one day with Him. But using the Apostle's statement as if it were a formula, just to make a point, we could say that only two of God's days have passed since the Lord Jesus was here the first time and promised to return. When scoffers ridicule the Second Coming of Christ, it might help us to look at the "delay" from God's viewpoint. It was only the day before yesterday that Jesus said He would come again. So, from that perspective, it really hasn't been that long at all!

When we see time from eternity's perspective, our heartaches, suffering, and tears seem to fade into insignificance. Our brief years are nothing when compared to the eternal glory that awaits every child of God. This kind of outlook helped the Apostle Paul to be a triumphant Christian in spite of his many trials. Though he had a painful "thorn in the flesh," spent many nights in jail, endured unmerciful floggings, suffered shipwreck, cold, and hunger, and even experienced the misunderstanding and opposition of his fellow Christians, he didn't give in to discouragement. He didn't complain; he didn't indulge in self-pity. Rather, he saw his earthly experiences as a prelude to eternal glory, and with that perspective he could bear them with joy. He wrote, "For our light affliction, which is but for a moment, worketh for us a far more exceeding and eternal weight of glory" (2 Cor. 4:17). He also said, "For I reckon that the sufferings of this present time are not worthy to be compared with the glory which shall be revealed in us" (Rom. 8:18).

If you are enduring a time of adversity, don't give in to discouragement. By faith, view your present afflictions in the light of eternity. It's the sure way to victory!

## God's Love for Man

The second answer Peter gave to help us be triumphant in the face of ridicule is that our Lord's "tarrying" is really a manifestation of His patient mercy. "The Lord is not slack concerning His promise, as some men count slackness, but is long-suffering toward us, not willing that any should perish, but that all should come to repentance" (2 Peter 3:9).

The Apostle was here exhorting believers not to look upon the apparent delay in Christ's return as an indication of divine heedlessness. On the contrary, we are to view His waiting so long as an indication of His love. When Peter said that the Lord "is longsuffering toward us, not willing that any should perish, but that all should come to repentance," he was reminding us of the mercy of God. You will notice that he spoke of it as being directed "toward us," the Lord's people. This means that Christ will not come back until all of His own, chosen in Him from before the foundation of the world (Eph. 1:4), have repented of their sins and accepted the Savior. Each day that He tarries, He gives sinners one more opportunity to respond to the message of saving grace.

Imagine that a father has promised his children a vacation in Washington, D.C., when they are all old enough to appreciate the meaning of what they will see there. They finally reach this stage of maturity, but the trip is delayed because the parents have become interested in a boy living in a foster home. They have set their love upon him and plan to adopt him as soon as necessary arrangements can be made. They don't believe it wise to divulge their reason for the postponement to their impatient children. But the day comes when the adoption procedure is finalized, and the youngster they were waiting for joins the family. Now they all take the trip. The family unit is complete. It was the mercy of the parents toward all their children—particularly this one little boy—which made the delay necessary. And the joy of everyone in the family was multiplied because there was now one more member of the family to share the expectation and fulfillment of the coming event.

God's patience encourages and consoles us as we wait for the return of His Son from heaven. Every passing day is a testimony of His love for mankind. When scoffers mock at Christ's seeming delay, we should tell them that it is only God's mercy that keeps Him from returning in wrath. For when the waiting is ended, it is *they* who will suffer in the judgment. God is not only being patient with us but also with them—giving them one more occasion to hear the Gospel. The Lord would be justified in sending down His fiery wrath upon our sinful race at any moment. But He delays, "not willing that any should perish, but that all should come to repentance."

### God's Sure Word of Prophecy
Having assured us that "the Lord is not slack concerning His promise," the Apostle went on to say, "But the day of the Lord will come as a thief in the night, in which the heavens shall pass away with

a great noise, and the elements shall melt with fervent heat; the earth also, and the works that are in it, shall be burned up" (2 Peter 3:10). To finite man, who is bound by the limitations of time, it may seem that the promise of the day of the Lord is a relic of the past. But we can know that He will surely come! God *keeps* His word! The Lord Jesus *is* coming again! Every prophecy concerning the events related to that great climactic occurrence are certain to be fulfilled.

What did Peter mean by the phrase, "the day of the Lord"? Expressions like the "day of the Lord," "that day," "the day," or "the great day" occur more than 95 times in the Bible, and the predominant idea is always judgment. We can summarize the teaching as follows: First of all, the Scriptures use the term "day of the Lord" to indicate the period of great tribulation that will be initiated by "the falling away" and the revealing of the "man of sin," the Antichrist (2 Thes. 2:3). Second, passages like Zechariah 14:1-4 portray the return of Christ in glory as the high point of the day of the Lord. Third, the kingdom of universal peace, righteousness, and prosperity to be established for 1,000 years at Christ's second coming is also referred to by this same designation.

This great day in God's prophetic program will begin without warning. It will come "as a thief in the night" (1 Thes. 5:2). The Lord Jesus Himself taught that just as the flood in Noah's day took that generation unawares, so also Christ's return will be totally unexpected. "But as the days of Noah were, so shall also the coming of the Son of man be. For as in the days that were before the flood they were eating and drinking, marrying and giving in marriage, until the day that Noah entered into the ark, and knew not until the flood came, and took them all away, so shall also the coming of the Son of man be" (Matt. 24:37-39). The element of surprise will characterize the coming of Jesus for His own at the Rapture, that great moment when He returns to defeat Antichrist and establish His kingdom. The same will be true of that time when He comes to crush the devil's final uprising at the close of the Millennium.

By the way, this should be a warning for all true believers in Christ to be leery of those who would set the date for the Lord's return. Someone is always saying, "The Lord will be coming within a few years," or even that He will come by a specific date. But they have no biblical authority to speak with certainty. Those who truly know the Lord Jesus are looking for His coming *every* day. I like this motto my father kept in his office: *Perhaps Today!*

Not only do we know that the day of the Lord will surely come, and that it will have an element of surprise, but we also believe that it will conclude with the cataclysmic destruction of our planetary system. The Bible says, "The heavens shall pass away with a great noise, and the elements shall melt with fervent heat; the earth also, and the works that are in it, shall be burned up" (2 Peter 3:10). This is graphic language indeed! It tells us that the entire earth system will be completely purged by fire in preparation for that pure and untainted new heaven and new earth, the final dwelling place of the redeemed. Therefore, the Apostle concluded this section by saying, "Nevertheless we, according to His promise, look for new heavens and a new earth, in which dwelleth righteousness" (2 Peter 3:13).

## The Day of the Lord Will Come

This section of Peter's epistle contains awesome prophetic statements. When God gives His word, He keeps it! We can therefore know with surety that the day of the Lord *will come.* In response to the skeptics who scoff at the Lord's return, we do well to keep in mind these three observations:

1. God's view of time. The Lord sees the events of a thousand years as clearly as He does those of one day (v. 8). He's not bound by the limitations of seconds and minutes and hours as we are. He observes all of the past, present, and future at once, and will return when His good pleasure dictates.

2. God's love for man. The delay in the Lord's return is really an expression of His patient mercy. "The Lord . . . is longsuffering toward us, not willing that any should perish" (v. 9). Those who ridicule Christ's return are in actuality the unknowing beneficiaries of His love. Were time to end before they received Christ, they would face certain doom.

3. God's prophetic declarations. The Lord means what He says. He is not "slack concerning His promise" (v. 9). From a human standpoint, the years keep passing by, but we know "the day of the Lord *will come*" (v. 10). We dare not forget it. In fact, we should always be ready for it.

## 2 Peter 3:11-14

Seeing, then, that all these things shall be dissolved, what manner of persons ought ye to be in
all holy living and godliness,

Looking for and hasting unto the coming of the
day of God, in which the heavens, being on fire,
shall be dissolved, and the elements shall melt
with fervent heat?

Nevertheless we, according to His promise,
look for new heavens and a new earth, in which
dwelleth righteousness.

Wherefore, beloved, seeing that ye look for
such things, be diligent that ye may be found of
Him in peace, without spot, and blameless.

# 12

# An Appropriate Life-style

The time is coming when the universe will disintegrate! The entire solar system, and our earth as we know it, is destined for destruction.

This is not merely the opinion of one pessimistic preacher—it's the accepted viewpoint of many respected men of science. Nuclear physicists, ecologists, and population experts foresee the day when life on earth will come to a cataclysmic end. And the Bible confirms their predictions! The Apostle Peter said, "The heavens shall pass away with a great noise, and the elements shall melt with fervent heat; the earth also, and the works that are in it, shall be burned up" (2 Peter 3:10). Unlike the non-Christian scientist, however, the Apostle doesn't leave us with the shattered remains of a once glorious world floating in the cold, empty darkness of space. He adds, "Nevertheless we, according to His promise, look for new heavens and a new earth, in which dwelleth righteousness" (2 Peter 3:13). This optimistic declaration presented clearly in Scripture, makes all the difference in the world!

Because of this bright prospect, the Christian can look forward with an attitude of confidence and hope. He sees his life as having meaning not only for the present but for eternity. In sharp contrast, the unbeliever has nothing to anticipate but hopelessness now and a bleak, foreboding existence beyond. No wonder so many atheists and agnostics cast away all moral restraint! No wonder they abandon themselves to the feverish pursuit of sinful pleasure! No wonder so many are slaves of alcohol and hallucinogenic drugs! We should not be surprised by the moral looseness, the drug addiction, and the suicides that mar our society. This behavior is the natural consequence of a despairing philosophy of life.

Every believer in Christ ought to be deeply grateful that God in His grace has reached a world of sinners with the truth. Right now Christ is preparing a bright future for us, and the anticipation of it should make a tremendous difference in the way we live. This reality should compel us to manifest a life-style that is in keeping with our view of the future glory that awaits us. There should be a detachment from the temporary things of earth, but there should also be an attachment to that which is spiritual and eternal.

Peter expressed both of these attitudes. We are told that the present earth system will disappear in a great rushing sound. It will be melted in torrid heat. But immediately we're confronted with the exclamation, "Seeing, then, that all these things shall be dissolved, what manner of persons ought ye to be in all holy living and godliness?" (2 Peter 3:11). Since we know that the earth will be destroyed by fire, how should we be living? In this passage the Apostle suggests four qualities that should mark the Christian who is ready for the last days:

1. An eager expectation.
2. A purposeful service.
3. A peaceful spirit.
4. A moral integrity.

Allow these four characteristics to bring your life into conformity with their pattern.

## An Eager Expectation

The first mark of a Christian looking for the return of Christ is an attitude of expectation and hope. "Looking for and hasting unto the coming of the day of God, in which the heavens, being on fire, shall be dissolved, and the elements shall melt with fervent heat" (2 Peter 3:12). We are to be watching for "the coming of the day of God." The Greek word *prosdokontas,* translated "looking for" in this verse, calls for an attitude of earnest anticipation. The same word was used by Luke in telling about the people who were eagerly awaiting Zacharias' reappearance after he had gone into the holy place of the temple to burn incense (Luke 1:21). It was used again (Acts 3:5) to describe the lame man who looked up pleadingly to Peter and John, fully expecting them to give him money. In the Book of Acts the word gives a striking picture of Cornelius and his friends as they anxiously waited for Peter to arrive and give them the message of the Gospel (Acts 10:24). When the Apostle spoke of believers as "looking for the coming of the day of God," he was saying that eager expectation is the quality which ought to mark every Christian as he looks for the fulfillment of biblical prophecy.

Peter's vivid language left no doubt as to what he meant. He went on, "In which the heavens, being on fire, shall be dissolved, and the elements shall melt with fervent heat" (2 Peter 3:12). But this does pose a problem. Why did he tell us to look forward to an event that is at least 1,000 years away? You see, the Bible teaches that the events surrounding the Second Coming, the Millennium, and the final rebellion of Satan against the Almighty, must take place before that day of fiery destruction. How much more sensible, one might ask, if Peter had encouraged us to look for the Lord's return? Why did he tell us to look for "the day of God"?

To answer this question, let me emphasize that every believer should be expecting Jesus Christ to return for His own. Yet we can be doing this and still be looking for that day when all sin and death shall be vanquished—the day of God that Peter mentioned here. Yes, we're exhilarated when we contemplate the translation of the Church, that moment when we meet the Savior in the air, and those glorious years when we'll reign with Him in the millennial kingdom! But remember, even during those 1,000 years the citizens of the earth will be living in physical bodies like ours. They will still possess a sinful nature. The children who are born to them will need to be saved, and apparently many people will render only an outward show of allegiance because they won't dare disobey.

The ultimate goal of God's program is a new world in which every vestige of sin is forever removed. In this chapter, therefore, Peter directed our eyes beyond the Second Coming, beyond the Millennium, beyond the devil's last rebellion, to that wondrous day when the new heavens and the new earth will be established in absolute perfection. *This* is what we should be anticipating.

## A Purposeful Service

The second mark of a believer who has a proper perspective of the last days is an involvement in serving the Lord that brings us closer to His coming. You see, as we witness and work for God, we actually hasten the return of Christ. Does that surprise you? If so, please read this, *"Looking for and hastening* the coming of the day of God, in which the heavens, being on fire, shall be dissolved, and the elements shall melt with fervent heat"* (2 Peter 3:12). In the first phrase of this verse the preposition "unto" tends to give a wrong impression. It does not appear in the original. Therefore, most grammarians render this segment, "Looking for and hasting unto the coming of the day of God." As we serve the Lord with diligence, therefore, we are helping to fulfill the prophetic Scriptures.

Some people in the past have erroneously thought that the entire world could be converted and the Millennium ushered in through evangelism and social action. They felt that an aggressive program of human self-improvement would create those conditions on earth that would be like the Millennium, and as a result, the Savior would come. This idea is foreign to the Scriptures. The Bible indicates that a worldwide rebellion against God will occur just before the Lord Jesus returns to establish His kingdom on the earth. But, we shouldn't take a defeatist attitude toward evangelism or missionary enterprise today. We don't know just when Jesus will come to take His own to heaven in the Rapture, so we cannot make specific predictions of what may or may not happen. But we do know that this catching away of the Church could take place at any moment, and that after this happens, conditions on earth will be marked by disaster and extreme wickedness for a brief period of time.

An evil ruler referred to as "the man of sin," "the son of perdition," "the beast," and "the Antichrist" will gain world power. He will do all he can to wipe out those who believe in God. For a time he'll be successful. But he and his armies will suffer a crushing defeat by the Lord Jesus at Armageddon when Christ returns from heaven as Lord of lords and King of kings. This will bring an end to the reign of darkness, and the kingdom of righteousness and peace will be established.

No, the Millennium will not be the product of human effort. Every Christian, however, can hasten the coming of the Lord by being a more effective soul winner. Then, when the last chosen saint of the Church age has been brought in, the Rapture will take place. And the sooner this occurs, the more quickly the final "day of God" will be ushered in. These truths should give us a great sense of purpose as we serve the Lord. They should motivate us to the kind of active labor for God that will hasten the coming of the end-time, and therefore bring closer the perfect glory of the new heavens and the new earth.

### A Peaceable Spirit

The third quality of the believer who has a proper attitude toward the future is a spirit that is at peace. Peter wrote, "Wherefore, beloved, seeing that ye look for such things, be diligent that ye may be found of Him in peace" (2 Peter 3:14). When the Apostle exhorted us to be found in peace, he very likely was speaking of our relationship with our fellowmen rather than with God.

Remember, he was addressing believers who were walking closely with the Lord. As Christians, we should also be relating successfully to others. We must avoid undue friction caused by a self-centered attitude. We must not throw grit into the machinery of human relationships by intolerance, anger, or an unforgiving spirit. We are to be *at peace* with our fellowmen.

The Bible emphasizes again and again our responsibility to have a peaceable spirit. In the Sermon on the Mount, the Lord Jesus said, "Blessed are the peacemakers; for they shall be called the sons of God" (Matt. 5:9). The writer of the Book of Hebrews said, "Follow peace with all men" (Heb. 12:14). We are also told, "the wisdom that is from above is first pure, then peaceable, gentle, and easy to be entreated, full of mercy" (James 3:17). And finally, the Apostle Paul declared, "the servant of the Lord must not strive, but be gentle unto all men" (2 Tim. 2:24).

A Christian who has detached himself from an improper love of the earthly and temporal, and has attached himself to that which is eternal and heavenly, is acting completely out of character if he becomes a troublemaker. When we realize that we're a dying people on a planet about to be destroyed, we'll not selfishly fight for fleeting fame or perishing riches—things that last only for a season. Yes, a peaceful spirit is a good way to show our longing for that which is to come and to make known our detachment from this world. Let's obey Peter's exhortation, "be diligent that ye may be found of Him in peace."

## A Moral Integrity
The fourth quality of a Christian prepared for

Christ's return is that of moral integrity. Our view of the future should result in a godly life here on earth. "Wherefore, beloved, seeing that ye look for such things, be diligent that ye may be found of Him in peace, without spot, and blameless" (2 Peter 3:14). The Apostle expected us to follow the example of Jesus. He used the same expression in his first epistle to describe Christ, "as of a lamb without blemish and without spot" (1 Peter 1:19). Purity, honesty, truthfulness, generosity, and the faithful performance of duty are among the virtues to be found in the life of the Christian who is ready for the Lord's return.

This will come naturally to the child of God as he looks "for new heavens and a new earth, in which dwelleth righteousness." Yearning for that time when sin will no longer be present to plague the world, he will endeavor to be holy and without sin right here and now. This is implied in the statement of the Apostle John, "Beloved, now are we the children of God, and it doth not yet appear what we shall be, but we know that, when He shall appear, we shall be like Him; for we shall see Him as He is. And every man that hath this hope in him purifieth himself even as He is pure (1 John 3:2-3).

## Watch and Pray

Believers who are looking forward to the coming of Christ and the promise of new heavens and a new earth will have the desire to be found "without spot, and blameless." Though they live in the midst of a sinful and Christ-rejecting world, they'll strive to attain the qualities of life that characterize the kingdom to follow. They'll endeavor to be now what they will be throughout eternity, diligently developing the traits that will be theirs in heaven.

Realizing that this world and everything in it will pass away, looking forward to new heavens and a new earth, and anticipating "that blessed hope" will give us a powerful incentive to lead a godly and holy life. We should be found praying, working, and watching as we await the return of Jesus Christ. We should try to conform our lives to what they will be in that day when all sin is vanquished and we are ushered into the very presence of the Lord Jesus.

## 2 Peter 3:13-18

Nevertheless we, according to His promise, look for new heavens and a new earth, in which dwelleth righteousness.

Wherefore, beloved, seeing that ye look for such things, be diligent that ye may be found of Him in peace, without spot, and blameless.

And account that the longsuffering of our Lord is salvation, even as our beloved brother, Paul, also according to the wisdom given unto him hath written unto you;

As also in all his epistles, speaking in them of these things, in which are some things hard to be understood, which they that are unlearned and unstable wrest, as they do also the other Scriptures, unto their own destruction.

Ye therefore, beloved, seeing that ye know these things before, beware lest ye also, being led away with the error of the wicked, fall from your own steadfastness.

But grow in grace, and in the knowledge of our Lord and Savior, Jesus Christ. To Him be glory both now and forever. Amen.

# 13

# Summing It Up

"Take care of yourself!"
"Don't forget to write!"
"Say hello to Grandma for me!"
Words of encouragement or advice like these always seem appropriate when you're about to close a letter or say good-bye to someone you love. When Peter came to the conclusion of his second epistle, he must have felt the same way, for he gave several parting admonitions in the final verses, and then concluded with a beautiful benediction.

## Be the Real Thing
The Apostle was concerned that his readers live in keeping with the glory of their salvation. He wanted them to be genuine, not hypocritical or artificial. He challenged them to develop the Christian graces of faith, virtue, knowledge, self-control, patience, godliness, brotherly kindness, and love (2 Peter 1:5-7). God had done His part in providing His people with full salvation; now they were to do their part by working it out through the development of these graces.

Continuing his exhortation, Peter told these believers to "make your calling and election sure." By this he meant that they were to confirm their divine call by living in a godly manner. A walk of genuine faith and obedience would give them inner security, keep them from stumbling, and offer evidence to their fellowmen that they were indeed members of God's family. Peter then promised that those who walked in obedience would be rewarded with an abundant entrance "into the everlasting kingdom of our Lord and Savior, Jesus Christ" (2 Peter 1:11). Our heavenly Father always responds positively to genuine trust and willing obedience—truths that should not be taken lightly. God hates sham but He loves sincerity. And He rewards all who faithfully follow Him.

## Accept the Apostolic Testimony

Peter's second command gave believers the responsibility for accepting the testimony of the apostles. After a brief reference to his impending death, Peter underscored the importance of remembering what he had been teaching them. What he and the other New Testament spokesmen had said and written was to be believed because it was based upon firsthand experience, and had been kept fresh in the minds of the Gospel writers through the ministry of the Holy Spirit. This is evidently what Peter was thinking as he penned these words: "Moreover, I will endeavor that ye may be able, after my decease, to have these things always in remembrance. For we have not followed cunningly devised fables when we made known unto you the power and coming of our Lord Jesus Christ, but were eyewitnesses of His majesty" (2 Peter 1:15-16).

This declaration takes on special significance in the light of the Apostle's age. At 60, he expected to die very soon as a martyr, for he wrote, "Knowing that shortly I must put off this my tabernacle, even as our Lord Jesus Christ hath shown me" (2 Peter 1:14). The Apostle may have been thinking of that day at the Sea of Tiberias when the resurrected Christ told him: " 'Verily, verily, I say unto thee, When thou wast young, thou girdedst thyself, and walkedst where thou wouldest; but when thou shalt be old, thou shalt stretch forth thy hands, and another shall gird thee, and carry thee where thou wouldest not.' This spoke He, signifying by what death he should glorify God. And when He had spoken this, He saith unto him, 'Follow Me' " (John 21:18-19).

Peter's reference to his decease make his words and his integrity become even more convincing. The Gospel story was not the result of the idle dreaming of idealistic men. The apostles believed strongly in the One they represented and suffered greatly for their faith. Tradition tells us that all but one of them died a martyr's death. Their testimonies were heartfelt, personal, and sincere. The person who rejects the truths they taught is guilty of denying willfully the very Word of the Lord. But on the other hand, the believer can have the wonderful confidence that his faith rests upon solid historical evidence! The writings and testimony of Peter and the others are genuine, and therefore *must* be accepted.

### Believe the Old Testament Scriptures

Peter's third exhortation was a call for belief in the Scriptures. Having referred to the reliability of his own experience with Christ, the Apostle pointed to the Old Testament as the basis of truth for the Christian faith. He was well aware that many of the people to whom he was writing knew about the prophecies that had been fulfilled in the birth, life, ministry, death, and resurrection of Jesus Christ. He reminded them that these Scriptures had originated with God, not with frail and erring men. Believers today, therefore, have more than the testimony of the apostles upon which to base their faith; they also have the witness of prophecies and their fulfillment.

## Beware of False Teachers

Peter's fourth admonition was to warn of false teachers. He said there had been false prophets in the past, and that many in the Church age would deny or distort the truths of God. We read, "But there were false prophets also among the people, even as there shall be false teachers among you, who secretly shall bring in destructive heresies, even denying the Lord that bought them, and bring upon themselves swift destruction" (2 Peter 2:1).

The Apostle continued his exhortation to watch out for false teachers by telling us what they are like (2 Peter 2:10-22). He graphically described their conduct as low and debased, referring to them as "natural brute beasts."

## Be Prepared for Scoffers

Peter's fifth imperative was that God's people should be prepared for mockers who would despise the teaching of Christ's return. This admonition stemmed from Peter's discussion of the second coming of Christ, and his mention of scoffers "walking after their own lusts." The Apostle pointed out that their disbelief and their scornful attitude would be the result of their willful rejection of the truth. Furthermore, he stated that their life-style would be selfish and evil—far different from that of true believers. Finally, he indicated that they would certainly experience God's wrath. Peter amplified by saying that these blasphemers would ignore history by not facing up to the truth that God had judged sin during past centuries. In addition, they would interpret Christ's apparent delay as a sign that He will never appear to right the wrongs of the ages.

The Apostle wrote all of this because he wanted us to be ready for opposition. Ridicule of Christ's return is prevalent today. Anyone who does much reading encounters snide remarks about the second coming of Jesus. But this shouldn't surprise us! Scoffers were present in the first century, and they've been around ever since. Peter said that we should be prepared for them.

## Live in the Light of the Day of God

The sixth imperative is the command to watch for and work toward the coming of the day of God. We may infer this from the Apostle's description of obedient believers who are "looking for and hasting unto the coming of the day of God" (2 Peter 3:12). The Apostle depicted a time when our entire universe shall pass away with a great noise and its elements melt in the fervent heat. What a frightening and awesome picture! God will have His day! No sinner will escape His wrath!

Living in the light of the coming of the day of God means doing all we can to reach people for Christ. It means being joyous and full of hope. It means being free from selfish materialism and living for the things of this world. It means keeping clean from the sins of the flesh. It means being serene in the face of adversity.

## Guard Against Falling

The seventh imperative is an admonition to guard against being led into sin and error. Peter wrote, "Ye therefore, beloved, seeing that ye know these things before, beware lest ye also, being led away with the error of the wicked, fall from your own steadfastness" (2 Peter 3:17). This exhortation follows Peter's reference to false teachers who were distorting the Scriptures, including those written by Paul. Apparently these heretics were twisting the doctrine of grace and confusing liberty with licentiousness. The Apostle Peter said that the Lord's people, having been warned, should not be deceived, nor let themselves fall into a pattern of life which would bring dishonor to Christ.

The words about being led away into error and falling from one's own steadfastness shall by no means be taken as an implication that a Christian can lose his salvation. Peter was only saying that a believer can fall from his place of spiritual stability. This happens all the time. Every church has had members who once stood for Christ, but who started slipping and eventually became backslidden. They were controlled by habits that marred their testimony and made them ineffective.

This kind of person is not at all happy. He believes in Christ, but he has no consciousness of God's presence. He lives in perpetual defeat, and his conduct is actually a hindrance to the cause of Christ. Unbelieving neighbors and fellow-workers see nothing in him that makes them want to become Christians. No victory. No joy. No transformation. But he is still saved, for the Scriptures make it crystal clear that a child of God will never lose his salvation and go to hell.

Every member of God's family has received a new nature, has the gift of the indwelling Holy Spirit, and has been made a citizen of heaven. This means that he can never be lost, but it does not inoculate him against being misled by false teachers. He can still fall into evil practices and lose the joy, peace, and effectiveness that ought to characterize every believer. He may have fallen from steadfastness, but not from his membership in God's family.

We must be on guard against men and women who do not teach the truth of God. We must be especially wary of those who come with novel ideas, claiming that they received them through some special revelation or vision. We must depend upon the Lord, study His Word, and determine to do His will. If we do these things, we will never become victims of false teachers.

## Grow in Grace

Having summarized the message of Peter's epistle, we come now to his parting exhortation: "But grow in grace, and in the knowledge of our Lord and Savior, Jesus Christ" (2 Peter 3:18). To grow in grace is to become more like the Lord Jesus, to grow in knowledge is to gain deeper understanding of Him and His redemption.

The call to "grow in grace" is in the present imperative verb tense, and could be translated, "keep on growing in grace." Life is never static. Every living thing in our universe, even the most simple form, is in a constant state of flux. The process of degeneration and renewal goes on all the time. The same is true in the spiritual realm.

It's impossible to maintain a spiritual *status quo;* if you don't grow, you retrogress. One of life's great tragedies is the Christian who, in his middle and older years, is less loving, less kind, less generous, less faithful, less gentle, and less self-controlled than he was right after his salvation. In direct contrast, one of the most beautiful things in the world is a believer who steadfastly, though perhaps not spectacularly, grows in Christian virtue and knowledge year after year. He becomes more and more like the Savior.

But I can imagine someone saying, "I agree with you. I *should* be growing in the grace and knowledge of the Lord Jesus. But I don't know how. Would you please tell me?" The best answer can be found in the laws that govern the physical and emotional development of a child. When his needs are met, he experiences a normal growth pattern. The same is true in the life of a believer.

First, the little one must be given adequate *nourishment.* Translating this into the spiritual realm, it means that the new believer must feed on the Scriptures. It's impossible to ignore the Bible and still become a strong Christian. Peter wrote, "As newborn babes, desire the pure milk of the word, that ye may grow by it" (1 Peter 2:2).

Second, a child needs *exercise* if he is to grow. A youngster kept in a small area day after day, week after week, will never develop properly nor reach his full potential. In the same way, the believer must exercise himself in an obedient walk and willing service.

No wonder some Christians never grow! They never *do* anything for the Lord. Oh, they may spend time reading the Bible, or may even take courses of study, but that's as far as it goes. They never apply it to their own lives. They refuse to obey its precepts. They don't share the Good News with others. How can they expect to grow? They can't because they are not getting any spiritual exercise.

The third essential in a child's development is *communication.* I feel sorry for those boys and girls whose parents never give them any attention. They often become socially maladjusted and have a difficult time finding their place in the world. Spiritually, the believer needs fellowship with his heavenly Father. He'll never develop into a strong, vibrant, mature Christian unless he communes with God in prayer and enjoys the blessing of His presence and guidance.

Fourth, a child needs *a friend*—someone he associates with who can help him grow into normal adulthood. This is also vital for the Christian. The author of Hebrews said, "And let us consider one another to provoke unto love and to good works, not forsaking the assembling of ourselves together, as the manner of some is, but exhorting one another, and so much the more, as ye see the day approaching" (Heb. 10:24-25).

To grow in grace and knowledge of the Lord Jesus Christ, therefore, you must feed on the Scriptures, walk in the pathway of obedience and service, spend time with God in prayer, and attend regularly a good, Bible-believing, Gospel-preaching church where you can enjoy the fellowship and support of other believers.

## To God Be the Glory
The Apostle concludes his epistle with a beautiful benediction focused upon Jesus Christ: "To Him be glory both now and forever. Amen" (2 Peter

3:18). What a tremendous way to close a letter! Yes, to Christ be the glory! And every believer in heaven and earth says "Amen" in response to this glorious finale of praise.

Others may not be able to sincerely join in saying that. They may not know the Lord Jesus as their Savior. Remember, He died to pay the price for sin. He arose from the grave to break the power of death. And salvation is offered to all who put their trust in Him. A decision for Christ should be made immediately. Those who have not accepted Christ might pray something like this: "Lord Jesus, I know that I'm a sinner. I believe You died for me. I receive You now as my Savior and Lord." If they really mean it, Christ *will* save them.

Jesus said, "I am the door; by Me if any man enter in, he shall be saved" (John 10:9). "To Him be glory both now and forever. Amen."